LAND ACKNOWLEDGEMENT

The earliest evidence of human culture on the Olympic Peninsula dates back almost 14,000 years: a spearhead lodged in a mastodon skeleton. The peoples of the maritime Northwest developed lifeways oriented, in many cases, toward the sea. Cedar longhouses and carved welcome figures marked settlements. Canoes plied extensive trade and hunting routes. Petroglyphs portrayed ships, killer whales, cosmological bodies and other symbols of a dynamic environment.

Today, eight Indigenous tribes have official associations with the national park: the Hoh, Jamestown S'Klallam, Lower Elwha Klallam, Makah, Port Gamble S'Klallam, Quileute, Quinault and Skokomish. Many other peoples of the region have current and historic ties to the Peninsula. With deep respect, we acknowledge all Indigenous peoples for whom this land holds significance.

"We come and go,
but the land is always here."

Willa Cather

They are America's shared inheritance. A reminder that this country belongs to the people. They are our best idea, an enduring connection to wild places as free as the air. Where we "wash our spirits clean," as John Muir wrote. Simply put, America's national parks summon us to the pursuit of happiness. The book in your hands is a celebration of these beautiful lands and their continued preservation.

Many thanks to our in-house Olympians: Ramona DeNies, Rebecca Jacobson and Jordan Kay in particular stuck with this project through a braided river of twists and turns. Gratitude, too, to Heron Scott at the Port Townsend School of Woodworking for a snapshot of high craft, and to Nikki McClure for explaining the dynamics of creative culture in her corner of the Peninsula. Loni Grinnell-Greninger expanded our perspective on Indigenous art.

WILDSAM FIELD GUIDES™

Published in the United States by Wildsam Field Guides, Austin, Texas.

Printed by TJ Books Ltd UK

ISBN 978-1-4671-9992-6

Illustrations by Jordan Kay

To find more field guides, please visit www.wildsam.com

CONTENTS

Explore Olympic National Park and the lands beyond

WELCOME

ON NEW YEAR'S EVE, 1889, six gentlemen partied in the woods of the Olympic Peninsula. They were called "the Press Expedition," after the Seattle newspaper sponsoring their mission. The menu: pea soup, boiled ham, baked beans, cornbread, prune pie and "deep potations of Java best."

Good that the explorers feasted then. They were about to spend six months in the Olympic Mountains, often living on "flour soup." Huge snowfalls, sinking rafts, donkeys plunging to doom: they learned why the Peninsula remained the West's most mysterious corner, guarded by dense forests and wild rivers. They also ran out of whiskey early on.

Yet when the Press Expedition emerged—bedraggled, but successful—their reports exalted beauty along with hardship. Milky torrents of glacier-fresh water. Moss, "bright with the sunshine of spring." Streams lively with trout, woods roamed by elk. Gleaming mountain lakes.

These intrepid fellows had discovered what Indigenous people had known for about 13,000 years. The Olympic Peninsula, practically an island squeezed between the ocean and Puget Sound, holds a world of its own, as generous as it is unforgiving. And, though this landscape faces the same challenges as the rest of our industrialized world, amazingly it abides to this day as place of wild promise, so close to Seattle that its mountains gleam on citydwellers' horizon. Most of the park is protected wilderness, and other designated wildlands circle the boundaries. No road cuts all the way through park's territory, meaning that the auto traveler of today must circle the edges via the huge loop of Highway 101. The wisest will stop for oysters at Hama Hama and Fjord Oyster Bank, bask in the sea air and gentility of Port Townsend, and venture out to La Push to catch a wave at First Beach. A night or two sheltering at Lake Quinault Lodge puts the modern roamer in touch with the woodsy nature-lovers of the 1920s.

So even the briefest outing into Olympic country mixes deep ecology and rooted culture. The Hoh Rainforest, the Shipwreck Coast, Mount Deception—the names alone resonate with mythic allure. The communities ringing the park have navigated these dramatic lands, rivers and seas, in some cases, for many centuries. If our national parks make a certain promise, this one might just deliver on it the best. Here at the edge of the continent, many wonders remain to explore. —The Editors

SELECTED CONTENT

Key facts, planning details and navigational aids to the national park and surrounding lands

PLANNING

GUIDES & OUTFITTERS

FISHING CHARTERS
Alpha Angler
La Push
alphaangler.com

GUIDED HIKES
Olympic Hiking Company
Port Angeles
hikeolympic.com

SEA KAYAK EXPEDITIONS
Adventures Through Kayaking
Port Angeles
atkayaking.com

MT. OLYMPUS SUMMIT
Miyar Adventures
Seattle
miyaradventures.com

BICYCLE RENTAL
The Broken Spoke
Port Townsend
thebrokenspoke.com

SURF INSTRUCTION
La Push Surf Adventures
La Push
lapushsurfadventures.com

BACKCOUNTRY SKI
Olympic Mountain Guiding
Sequim
olympicmountainguiding.com

CLIMATE

Twelve feet of rain. What does that even look like? That's the annual precipitation scorecard for the Hoh Rainforest, the wettest place in the continental United States. Perhaps it's easier to grasp what this trophy deluge *feels* like: Dense lushness, soft and gauzy, the sensation of being bathed in neon color. Olympic also takes in coastlands, storm-tossed in winter and temperate in summer, and snowcapped alpine heights. Wherever, whenever, pack your waterproofs.

CALENDAR

JAN Storm watching & king tides
FEB Winter steelhead fishing
MAR Prime elk spotting
Best surf waves, Westport
APR Olympic BirdFest
Viking Fest, Poulsbo
MAY Sequim Irrigation Festival
JUN Baby marmot season
JUL Quiluete Days, La Push
Gravel Unravel bike race
AUG Makah Days, Neah Bay
SEP Olympia Zine Fest
Wooden Boat Fest
OCT Dungeness Crab Fest, Port Angeles
NOV Geoducks basketball
DEC Ski season opens, Hurricane Ridge

BOOKING

Notes on navigation and Olympic pursuits.

VISITOR CENTERS

Port Angeles is HQ. Hoh Rainforest and Hurricane Ridge also have centers, and ranger stations operate seasonally. *nps.gov/olym*

BACKCOUNTRY

All overnight trips into the park wilds require permits. Summer bookings open on April 15 each year. *recreation.gov*

QUOTA ZONES

Select areas limit the number of backcountry permits, such as Sol Duc, Seven Lakes Basin and Cape Alava. 360-565-3100

CAMPGROUNDS

Some of 14 official campgrounds are first-come-first-served all the time; others require permits in summer. *recreation.gov*

LODGES

Lake Quinault and Kalaloch are open year-round. Sol Duc, Lake Crescent and Log Cabin Resort run spring-fall. *nps.gov/olym*

MOUNT OLYMPUS

With 3 to 4 days needed to reach the peak, wilderness permits are required. USGS Olympus map recommended. *mountaineers.org*

TRADITIONS

Cultural practices rooted in the Olympic Peninsula.

Native Art	Striking geometries, bold graphic sensibility and stark color-blocking typify Indigenous art of the Peninsula and islands to the north. *Northwest Native Expressions, Sequim*
Wooden Boats	Traditional canoes of the Makah and other tribes continue to ply Olympic waters. Port Townsend is a hub of boat-building and repair. *Haven Boatworks, Port Townsend*
Indie Rock	Kurt Cobain famously hailed from gritty Aberdeen. Olympia, hometown of Sleater-Kinney and riot grrrl, remains a hotbed of rebel sound. *K Records, Olympia*
Oystering	Building on ancient Indigenous aquaculture, cultivators produce briny beauties: Sequim Bay jades, Baywater sweets, etc. *Jamestown Seafood, Sequim*

HISTORY

Humans have lived on and around the Olympic Peninsula for at least 13,000 years. Events of more recent centuries:

1600s...Mudslide partially buries Makah village at Ozette
1774.....Juan Perez, sailing for Spain, becomes the first European to document the Olympic Peninsula and surrounding islands
1778.....Captain James Cook ventures to Northwest, part of final voyage
1788..... Meares, British captain and mountebank, names Mount Olympus
1805..... Lewis & Clark Expedition reaches mouth of the Columbia
1808.... Russian vessel *SV Nikolai* runs aground. Confrontations with Hoh and Makah tribes
1811......Astoria established: U.S. outpost, beaver-trade hub
1818.....U.S. and Britain agree on joint occupation of "Oregon Country"
1834.....Makah encounter Japanese castaways, the "Three Kichis"
1846....Britain and U.S. divide Northwest claims; Strait of Juan de Fuca is maritime border. Oregon Territory formed two years later.
1853......Washington Territory created, with Olympia as capital
1855-6..Series of treaties: Point-No-Point, Neah Bay, Olympia. Native lands reduced, reservations established.
1890.....Seattle *Press* sponsors expedition to Olympic interior
1897.....Olympic Forest Reserve [future national forest] established
1909.....Teddy Roosevelt declares Mount Olympus National Monument
1920s...Makah Tribe voluntarily ends traditional whale hunts
1924.....Aberdeen declares itself "Lumber Capital of the World"
1926.....Lake Quinault Lodge: example of "Park Rustic" style
1938.....Franklin Roosevelt responds to calls to preserve primordial forests, supporting Olympic National Park creation
1942-3..World War II coastal defenses built within national park
1952.....Hurricane Ridge Lodge dedicated
1966.....Archaeological excavations begin at Ozette
1974.....Boldt Decision: landmark ruling affirming tribal fishing rights
1997..... Heaviest rain year ever in Forks: 162 inches
..... Olympic National Park visitation record: 3.8 million
1999..... Makah Tribe stages successful whale hunt after court battle
2005.... Single red pebble marks "One Square Inch of Silence" along Hoh Rainforest trail
2008.... Wild Olympics campaign to expand wilderness areas launched
2011..... Elwha River dam removal begins, restoring salmon habitat

MEDIA

MUSIC

Nirvana
Neko Case
Black Belt Eagle Scout
Beat Happening
Brandi Carlile
Sleater-Kinney
Karl Blau
Bikini Kill
Wolves in the Throne Room
Unwound

ARTISTS

Randy Capoeman
Silkscreen printing

Young Doctor
Woodcarving

Mary Randlett
Photography

Maria Coryell-Martin
Conceptual art

Orré Nobles
Art colony founder

BOOKS

☞ *The Last Wilderness* by Murray Morgan. One of the Northwest's great yarnspinners, Morgan reels off a rough-and-tumble history of the Peninsula, long on characters and incident. Grab a pint for this one.

☞ *The Egg and I* by Betty MacDonald. A bestseller back in 1945, this jaunty memoir chronicles the haphazard life of a Chimicum farm family. If you've heard tell of "Ma and Pa Kettle," this book started it.

☞ *The Sea is My Country: The Maritime World of the Makahs* by Joshua L. Reid. A distinguished historian [and Snohomish tribal member] plumbs deep Makah influence on the Northwest's evolution.

☞ *Collected Stories* by Raymond Carver. With a life lived between an Oregon logging town and Port Angeles [and, sure, places in between], the short-story master defined a flinty, tragic and wry outlook.

☞ *Hunger Makes Me a Modern Girl* by Carrie Brownstein. The Sleater-Kinney guitar ace tells an archetypal Pacific Northwest youth-culture story, delving into the creative ferment of Olympia.

☞ *Olympic National Park: A Natural History* by Tim McNulty. An acclaimed go-to on the park's landscape and biology, weaving together plants, animals, human culture, the deep past and challenged future of this critical ecological sphere.

LODGING

TOWN BASE
Bishop Hotel
Port Townsend
thebishophotel.com
The rooms: vintage Victoriana. The lobby: sparkly mod café/bottleshop.

WATERSIDE
Mike's Beach Resort
Hood Canal
mikesbeachresort.com
Bunk down on the literal bank of the fjord, then scuba to spy wolf eels and the giant octopus.

DEEP IN THE WOODS
Hoh Valley Cabins
Near Forks
hohvalleycabins.com
Modular modern pods sprinkled in a rainforest clearing, with quick access to hiking trails.

DELUXE RUSTIC
Mossquatch Resort
Near Forks
mossquatchresort.com
Rustic cabins and glampy tents bring the funk. Group site available, too.

FAR CORNER
Hobuck Beach Resort
Neah Bay
hobuckbeachresort.com
Makah Tribe-run cabins, as far northwest as you can go.

BEACHFRONT
Quileute Oceanside Resort
La Push
quileuteoceanside.com
Vibe out to the First Beach surf beat.

OCEAN CABINS
Kalaloch Lodge
Near Forks
thekalalochlodge.com
Hard to get closer to the Pacific than these rows of trim abodes. Numbers 6, 7 and 8 are the top draft picks.

GATEWAY TOWN
Olympic Lodge
Port Angeles
ayershotels.com
Generous breakfast for dawn-patrol runs to Lake Crescent or Hurricane Ridge.

VINTAGE TRAILERS
The Sou'Wester
Seaview
souwesterlodge.com
Coming to or going from the Peninsula, this village of mid-century ramblers is a PNW cult fave.

FARM-TO-TABLE REFUGE
Tokeland Hotel
Toke Point
tokelandhotel.com
Oldest hotel in WA, now the domain of cookbook author Heather Earnhardt.

OLD NORTHWEST
The Arctic Club
Seattle
arcticclubhotel.com
Throwback to days of ship's captains and gold-rush gamblers. Incredible walrus gargoyles.

ISLAND LODGE
Captain Whidbey
Whidbey Island
captainwhidbey.com
Time capsule of woodsy style, just a ferry ride away from Port Townsend.

SIDE TRIPS

Public lands and other unique experiences beyond the park's borders.

VICTORIA, BRITISH COLUMBIA

The historic Black Ball Line sets sail from Port Angeles for Vancouver Island and this beguiling city's combination of retro-Anglophilia and modern Canada: ornate Parliament, farm-to-table nirvana. *cohoferry.com*

DUNGENESS NATIONAL WILDLIFE REFUGE

A thin curl of land, one of the world's longest sand spits, shelters biologically rich waters and provides a weighstation for migrating birds. Scope out sinister Graveyard Spit. *fws.gov*

LEADBETTER POINT STATE PARK

One of the more fascinatingly out-there, precarious spots on the West Coast: the very tip of the rail-thin Long Beach Peninsula, with Pacific waves on one side and vast Willapa Bay on the other. *parks.wa.gov*

THE HIGH STEEL BRIDGE

Real good truth in naming on this one. Originally the tallest railroad bridge in the U.S., this 1929 truss span soars 365 feet above the Skokomish River below: an unforgettable, if woozy, view. *Forest Service Rd #2340.*

DOSEWALLIPS STATE PARK

For a vintage experience of gritty Puget Sound beach culture, seek the clams [Manila and native little necks], oysters and mysterious geoducks at this shellfish-foraging site. Check the regs and safety notes. *wdfw.wa.gov*

SAN JUAN ISLANDS

A dreamy archipelago, a scattering of emerald isles in the misty seas at America's edge ... it's not hard to get poetic about the San Juans. Take a ferry to these outposts for artsy towns and orca-spotting. *Embark at Anacortes*

OLYMPIC DISCOVERY TRAIL

Iconic among cyclists in the Northwest, this 135-mile path links Port Townsend and La Push, sometimes threading along beaches and bays, other times plunging into the National Park's dense woods. *olympicdiscoverytrail.org*

ISSUES

Wilderness	Many years in the making, a bill to expand the protected wilderness areas around the park boundaries is crawling through the halls of Congress. Opponents fear negative economic effects. **EXPERT:** *Connie Gallant, chair, Wild Olympics*
Whaling	In 1999, the Makah Tribe famously conducted its first traditional whale hunt in many decades. Since then, whaling has been back on hold, as a complex process of environmental review triggered by the tribe's desire to exercise its treaty rights unfolds. As of 2024, many expect a ruling ... sometime. **EXPERT:** *Timothy J. Greene Sr., chairman, Makah Tribe*
Economy	Aberdeen and other towns around the park's perimeter owed past prosperity to the timber trade. The industry's decline in recent decades left a legacy of longterm distress. Tourism and new exports [soybeans, e.g.] provide opportunity but not the bedrock blue-collar economy of old. **EXPERT:** *Erik Larson, former mayor, Aberdeen*
Climate	Forged by torrential rains, temperate seasons and glacial ice, Olympic is, of course, vulnerable to climate change. Decreased precipitation, declining glaciers and larger, more numerous fires count among the symptoms. **EXPERT:** *Jessica Halofsky, director, Northwest Climate Hub*

STATISTICS

18.33 .... Average winter-month rainfall, Hoh Valley [inches]
1.6 .... Average winter-month rainfall, Sequim [inches]
25 .... Max. length [cm.]: banana slug, world's second-largest slug
4,846 .... Deepest point in underwater Quinault Canyon [ft.]
75,000 .... Initial print run of *Twilight*, Forks vampire epic, 2005
250 .... Deer within Port Townsend limits, 2022 [undercount suspected]
3 .... Ski areas with lifts in national parks, including Hurricane Ridge

EXPERTISE

MAKAH CARVING
Micah McCarty
@klaowus
Astonishing works in cedar, carved in Neah Bay. Evoking centuries of Makah history; pointing to the future.

SAILING INSTRUCTION
Northwest Maritime Center
nwmaritime.org
Voyages off Port Townsend, basic keelboats to the majestic *Vie en Rose*.

FORAGER
Langdon Cook
@langdoncook
Seattle-based hunter of mushrooms, writer of books and advocate for wild shellfish habitat in the Sound.

BASKETWEAVING
Harvest Moon
iamharvestmoon.com
Quinault storyteller and cultural ambassador, steeped in the meaning behind the art and craft.

SALMON RECOVERY
Joe Anderson
wdfw.wa.gov
Studying the hope and complexity of the mighty chinook's recovery after dam removal on the Elwah River.

FLOTSAM
Beachcombers' Alert
beachcombersalert.org
Singular, sharp-eyed Seattle-based newsletter on ocean-borne debris.

DRIFTWOOD SCULPTURE
Tuttie Peetz
olympicdriftwoodsculptors.org
A luminary of a booming driftwood subculture, crafting flowing forms and teaching classes in Sequim.

BIGFOOT
Rich Germeau
olympicproject.com
After a four-second encounter of his own, a dedicated researcher of the Sasquatch question.

WOODWORKING
Port Townsend School of Woodworking
ptwoodschool.org
Honing technique and aesthetic vision, for amateurs and aspiring pros alike.

SHIP'S CAPTAIN
Alex Wilken
seattleboatworks.com
Lifelong sailboat skipper leads all manner of charters.

OUTDOOR FEASTS
Windward Adventures
windwardadventures.com
Destination dinners and guided multi-day trips in search of local foodstuffs. Hoh Valley outing.

CONSERVATION
Sarah Spaeth
saveland.org
Northwest lifer helping guide Jefferson Land Trust preservation projects: Duckabush, Dosewallips, others.

INCLUDING

NATURAL WORLD

A field guide to plants, wildlife and landscapes across the park, including bits of history, curiosities and current issues

LAND

ONE PARK, THREE ECOSYSTEMS

A geographical and ecological pivot point for the continent's North Pacific coast, Olympic National Park embraces several landscapes within its 1,400-plus square miles. Some have called this domain "three parks in one."

THE MOUNTAINS The Olympic Mountains are among the world's most precipitous rises, vaulting abruptly from sea level to 8,000 feet at Mount Olympus' summit. This creates a rain shadow, leaving lands to the east much drier than the drenched west. Unlike other Northwestern peaks [Rainier, St. Helens], the Olympics are not volcanoes. Rather, they could be described as crumpled seafloor, mashed upward by tectonic forces.

THE COAST In a geopolitical anomaly, a thin thread of national park extends out of the park's core to include 73 miles of ocean shore. Some of the most isolated beaches on the American West Coast, these are tumultuous places, lashed by high tides and horizontal rains in winter.

THE RAINFOREST Famed as the home to "the quietest place in America," the Olympics' temperate rainforest can feel like Earth at its most Earth-like. The Hoh Rainforest is the nation's wettest, soaking up more than 130 inches annually. Gigantic trees, moss, kaleidoscopic lichen—this is plant paradise, and also a cradle of animal life, ranging from the humble banana slug to the majestic Roosevelt elk.

WILDERNESS

A great portion of the national park is designated as wilderness, meaning no roads, wheeled vehicles or new human structures. The park's Daniel J. Evans Wilderness also borders protected wildlands in the national forest: the Buckhorn, Brothers, Mount Skokomish, Wonder Mountain and Colonel Bob wilderness areas.

WILD RIVERS

The defining link between the high country and stormy seas.

The arms of an octopus. Spokes of a wheel. Metaphors for the pinwheel of rivers that pour down from the Olympics' mountainous core vary. Study the map and one essential from a human point of view becomes obvious: flowing waters carve the only viable paths into the forests and mountains, and most roads and trails here trace their banks. The peninsula's tight, island-like geography means rivers drop rapidly from their headwaters to the ocean—some are among the world's steepest rivers. Of age-old importance to the region's Indigenous peoples, today the Olympic rivers are also notable as an ecological refuge, with their headwaters and much of their flow enjoying national park protection. In recent years, advocates have urged formal Wild & Scenic designations and further safeguards, but the politics are still unfolding. Several highlights of this complex watershed:

HOH Arguably the most popular Olympic river among anglers seeking salmon, trout and steelhead, this 56-mile, glacier-fed flow often attains a mystical emerald-milk hue. In the Quileute language spoken by the Hoh tribe: Cha'lak'at'sit ["Southern River"]; it meets the sea on the Hoh Reservation.

DUNGENESS Twenty-eight miles long, the Dungeness threads through the Buckhorn Wilderness, its plunge abrupt enough to stir esteemed but challenging whitewater. September's Dungeness River Festival celebrates the ecosystem.

HAMMA HAMMA The river so nice, they named it twice. [Actually, the name derives from an ancestral Twana village.] Drops 5,000 feet in 15 miles, with notable waterfalls, trout fishing.

SOL DUC At 78 miles, the longest river originating in the park. From Sol Duc Hot Springs a 1.6-mile trail reaches Sol Duc Falls, one of the park's signature sights. As it nears the sea, the Sol Duc combines with the Bogachiel River to form the Quillayute. Mora Campground and Rialto Beach are near at hand.

THE OLYMPIC RANGE

From rainforest lowlands to snowbound ridges, the Olympic Mountains rise from the Pacific Ocean to their highest summit on glacial Mount Olympus. Composed of 244 mountains—and those are just the named ones—the range presents many climatic zones and ecosystems, from western sea coast to where the range meets Puget Sound in the east, then on to the Strait of Juan de Fuca up north.

MOUNT OLYMPUS .... 7,980 ft
Tallest mountain on the peninsula, king of the range

MOUNT ZION .... 4,278 ft
Fir, cedar and towering groves of wild rhododendron

THE BROTHERS .... 6,842 ft
Experts get to this pair through old growth and forested canyon

MOUNT DECEPTION .... 7,788 ft
A steep rise above Royal Basin

MOUNT SKOKOMISH .... 6,434 ft
Home to mountain goats, three epic summits

MOUNT WALKINSHAW .... 7,378 ft
Northernmost peak in the subset "Needles" range

BOGACHIEL PEAK .... 5,474 ft
Views of Mount Olympus and the Blue Glacier across the Hoh Valley

HURRICANE RIDGE .... 5,242 ft
Super accessible [and plentiful] meadow and ridge trails

HAL FOSS PEAK .... 7,179 ft
Bare, rugged terrain and glacial landscape

MOUNT TOWNSEND .... 6,243 ft
Wildflower meadows, secret waterfalls, turtleback summit

MOUNT ELLINOR .... 5.952 ft
Relaxed switchbacks and Lake Cushman views

MOUNT ROSE .... 4,301 ft
Hikers trek year-round for peekaboo sightings of Mount Rainier

MOUNT GLADYS .... 5,600 ft
Gentle counterpoint to tougher neighbors Cruiser, Lincoln, Henderson

SEA STACKS

Rocky pillars standing in the ocean not far from shore, sea stacks are the dramatic remnants of headlands torn from the mainland and sculpted by the erosive power of wind and waves. Winter storms can bring winds up to 150 miles per hour and waves up to 90 feet in height, and these jagged landforms have long presented perilous obstacles to mariners: some 200 shipwrecks have been recorded on the Olympic coast since 1810. But for large colonies of seabirds—cormorants, auklets, storm-petrels, murres, gulls, puffins—they serve as refuge and nesting grounds. For foraging sea lions and seals, they are vital haul-out sites. To spy a particularly spectacular display, hike to sandy Shi Shi Beach and continue along the water's edge to a mile-long stretch of stacks known as Point of the Arches. Round trip is about 8 miles; note that a Makah tribal recreation permit is required in addition to a park pass. Rialto Beach, Second Beach and Ruby Beach also feature notable examples. A modern-classic treatment of the peninsula's landscape can be found in Rowland W. Tabor's *Guide to the Geology of Olympic National Park* [1st ed., 1975].

FLORA

WILDFLOWERS OF NOTE

OLYMPIC VIOLET *Viola flettii* Tiny lavender blooms—endemic to the Olympic Mountains—burst forth in early summer and are found nowhere else on earth.

AVALANCHE LILY *Erythronium montanum* The first snow melt reveals a meadow carpet of creamy, feather-edged flowers with showy, butter-yellow centers.

QUEEN'S CUP *Clintonia uniflora* This rhizomatous perennial grows in the understory of northern coniferous forests and boasts a single amethyst berry and pearly florescence.

ROCKFOIL *Saxifraga* Dense, low-growing foliage and vibrant-hued saucer blooms are tenacious cover for wet zones, rocks, shady nooks.

GREEN HELLEBORE *Helleborus viridis* Touching [or eating] the leaves, sepals or out-of-this-world acid-green flower stems elicits a toxic response, ranging from skin rash to a slowed heartbeat.

RED COLUMBINE *Aquilegia formosa* Spurred flowers in ruby and lemon hang lantern-like, attracting hummingbirds and humans; the nectar was eaten as a candy by the Gitxsan and Wet'suwet'en peoples. Aquila—"eagle"—refers to a petal shape that resembles an eagle's talons.

PINK COAST RHODODENDRON *Rhododendron macrophyllum* Found at low elevation along roadsides and in rainshadow, flamboyant trusses of candy-colored blooms reach as high as 24 feet.

SCARLET PAINTBRUSH *Castilleja coccinea* The crimson calyx of this herbaceous mountain dweller was used by Indigenous peoples to ease the discomforts of rheumatism—and as an aphrodisiac.

SITKA VALERIAN *Valeriana sitchensis* In damp, subalpine meadows luxuriant growths of these aromatic white blooms rest on tall stalks; ancient origins in treating insomnia and nervous disorders.

MOSSES AND LICHENS

Green. Green. Green. First visual impressions of the Olympic forests vibrate in neon greens, psychedelic in intensity. This is because the woods' fertility and sheer dampness make this peninsula one of Earth's great habitats for moss. While "simple" in structure—no seeds, leaves or vascular structures—these "cryptograms" form a complex base layer for biological diversity. A 2005 scientific survey revealed more than 13,000 species in the park: a forest within a forest, on a small, plush scale. Look out for stairstep moss building up over last year's growth, and club moss, draping and bearding [no other word for it] rainforest trees in extravagant fashion. While Olympic's moss mosaic plays many ecological roles, a notable function manifests when a tree falls dead. Mosses tend to be the first colonists of fallen trunks, forming layers of fertility that seeds then exploit to sprout newborn trees. Lichens, another genre of cryptogram, likewise blanket the park. Fascinatingly, lichen are not singular organisms but rather collaborations between algae and fungi or bacteria. In the 1970s, botanists discovered that the lichen *Lobaria oregana* plays a key role in Olympic ecosystems, harvesting atmospheric nitrogen up in the forest canopy, then drifting down, nearly invisible, to deliver that nitrogen to the forest floor's soil.

COMMON FERNS

SWORD FERN
Polystichum munitum
Typical frond of the Olympic forest floor. Leathery, toothy, at home in the cool and wet.

LADY FERN
Athyrium filix-femina
Possibly named for its delicate, lacy construction. Thrives in moist forest and swampy spots.

LICORICE FERN
Polypodium glycyrrhiza
Can grow up the sides of moss-laden trees; especially in love with bigleaf maples.

PACIFIC OAK FERN
Gymnocarpium disjunctum
Found in shady, moist spots—streambanks, misty cliffs. Prefers coniferous woodlands.

TREES OF NOTE

WESTERN RED CEDAR *Thuja plicata*

Culturally crucial to Northwest tribes for its uses in building, boatmaking and many arts, this titanic species thrives in the Olympian wet, but also grows well in drier climes. Confusingly, not really a cedar, if we're getting technical, but the largest member of the separate *Thuja* genus. The peninsula is home to some astonishing giants—some of which have fallen to natural causes in recent years. The Quinault Big Cedar went down in a 2016 storm; ill winds split the Kalaloch Big Cedar in 2014, though it still stands. Groves of huge trees, however, remain.

SITKA SPRUCE *Picea sitchensis*

The largest spruce species and one of the biggest trees on the planet, the Sitka's ancestral range runs from Northern California up to Alaska. A sobering history of logging has reduced its footprint in today's world, but the Olympic Peninsula shelters some heroic examples—indeed, the largest known Sitka stands near Lake Quinault, less than half a mile down a well-traveled trail.

DOUGLAS FIR *Pseudotsuga menziesii*

Arguably the definitive tree of the Pacific Northwest, this mega-conifer is not a true fir. Nor a pine, nor a hemlock. Hence, the "pseudo" in a scientific name that also pays homage to the Scottish botanist Archibald Menzies, an early 19th century figure who introduced the monkey puzzle tree to Britain. The English-language name salutes another Scot, explorer and botanist David Douglas, who came to a murky end in Hawai'i—but that's another story. The Queets Fir, the world's largest by diameter, looms over the Queets River Trail.

BIGLEAF MAPLE *Acer macrophyllum*

Many of the mystical, moss-draped limbs and trunks that define the visual palette of the Olympic rainforests belong to this, the largest of maple trees. The Maple Glade Nature Loop, a gentle half-mile loop from the Quinault, showcases the species in its Olympic mode.

For a vintage report on Olympic logging, see The Final Forest *by William Dietrich* [1992, *updated* 2011].

Western Red Cedar
Sitka Spruce
Douglas Fir

FAUNA

NATIVE SPECIES OF NOTE

OLYMPIC MARMOT *Marmota olympus* Playful rodents, bushy of tail, brownish of hue [lighter after hibernation]. Grow to around 15 pounds and live above 4,000 feet in elevation.

OLYMPIC TORRENT SALAMANDER *Rhyacotriton olympicus* Breathing partly through brown-colored skins, they flip to show yellow bellies when facing predators.

BURRINGTON JUMPING SLUG *Hemphillia burringtoni* Yes, these land slugs "jump," coiling bodies to break their slime trails and throw off predators. Important role in recycling organic matter.

OLYMPIC CHIPMUNK *Tamias amoenus caurinus* Tiny mammals, less than a pound, bear classic chipmunk markings: striped backs, white bellies, sometimes food-stuffed cheeks.

SHORT-TAILED WEASEL *Mustela erminea olympica* Olympic weasels don't turn white before hibernation. Brownish with yellow underbelly, long, svelte and strong, they can eat bigger rodents as well as hares.

QUILEUTE GAZELLE BEETLE *Nebria acuta quileute* Brown antennae and legs poke from shiny black backs with ridges running longwise.

HULBIRT'S SKIPPER *Hesperia comma hulbirti* Butterfly from the Hesperiidae family has a greenish-brown body, wings with white-golden spots.

OLYMPIC MUDMINNOW *Novumbra hubbsi* Washington's only known endemic freshwater fish grows to about 3 inches and thrives in dense vegetative waters and mud beds.

OLYMPIC POCKET GOPHER *Thomomys mazama melanops* Hard to spot, as they mostly live underground [pocket gophers are the only true subterranean rodents in North America]. Brown bodies, small eyes and ears.

SALMON

When an adult male salmon returns to fresh water after years at sea, he usually stops eating. He has one goal: to return to where he was born, spawn and die. His body is already decaying. But he still needs to fight off other males, so he grows fangs and a hooked snout called a kype: the source of the genus name *Oncorhynchus*, from the Greek. Salmon are athletes: pushing up rivers against the current, torpedoing over cascades. And they're ancient, evolving from a common ancestor as late as 20 million years ago, when gingko trees fanned across Washington under clouds of volcanic ash. In Olympic rivers like the Quillayute, Quinault and Hoh, all seven Pacific salmonid species are present, including cutthroat trout and steelhead. But they exist at a fraction of the numbers seen here even 70 years ago. Declines mainly stem from 150 years of overfishing, mining and logging, plus dams and other roadblocks. Today, the tribes of Olympic Peninsula co-manage salmon fisheries with Washington State. They set strict harvest rules, including "escapement"—how many salmon must reach spawning grounds before fishing can start. Some tribes maintain hatcheries to boost their catch. Yet these measures may not be enough. Ozette Lake sockeye are now protected under the Endangered Species Act, as are Hood Canal summer chum and Puget Sound Chinook. But salmon are also survivors, enduring ice ages, floods and eruptions. On the Olympic Peninsula, fishery managers are giving salmon more space, even tearing down dams; before 2014, two loomed over the Elwha River inside Olympic National Park. Already, thousands of salmon are back.

OCEAN GARDENS

From the air, a sharp eye tracing the Hood Canal might spot ancient Coast Salish infrastructure, some older than Egypt's pyramids. At the low tide mark, low rock walls terrace beaches. These are clam gardens: mariculture practiced from what is now northern Washington State to Southeast Alaska. This ancestral technology can more than triple a clam bed's productivity. And it's making a comeback, thanks in part to groups like the Pacific Sea Garden Collective and the Clam Garden Network. Skye Augustine [Hwsyun'yun], a Hul'q'umi'num' adviser with Parks Canada, has coordinated restorations in the North Salish Sea. "I'm excited to see them full of life," she told Yes! *magazine in 2017. "Full of clams and people digging, laughing, telling stories, learning together."*

MOLLUSKS OF NOTE

FOOLISH MUSSEL *Mytilus trossulus* Tide chart, bucket, flathead screwdriver: a mussel hunter's friends. On Hood Canal, foolish mussels encrust reefs from Hope Island to Shine Tidelands. Check safety, seasons first [wdfw.wa.gov/licenses]. Later, *moules frites*.

NUTTALL'S COCKLE *Clinocardium nuttallii* Also known as a "heart" or "basket" cockle, this smaller, rounder clam cousin has a mottled shell, ribbed like a fan from its hinge. Prized for milder, less briny flavor.

GEODUCK *Panopea generosa* From the Coast Salish word g^{w}*ídəq*, or "dig deep," the world's largest burrowing clam—think a three-pound elephant trunk in a tiny shell—can live more than 150 years. Millions of geoducks ["gooey-ducks"] blanket the bottom of Puget Sound.

GOOSE BARNACLE *Pollicipes polymerus* With a pearlescent leafed helmet and black swan neck, this strange crustacean is as bizarre as the myths that surround it. Look for these "dinosaur feet" [*percebes*, as they're known in elite cuisine] wedged between mussels in tidelands.

GUMBOOT CHITON *Cryptochiton stelleri* Wearing a fiery red mantle over eight armored plates, the giant Pacific chiton can surpass a foot in length. It's been called a wandering meatloaf. Theoretically, you can eat it—once you get past its retractable teeth, made of rock-hard magnetite.

OLYMPIA OYSTER *Ostrea lurida* The West Coast's only native oyster is petite, the size of a small egg, and now dangerously rare. Coveted in the gold rush, "Olys" gave us the 12-oyster Hangtown Fry.

PACIFIC LITTLENECK CLAM *Leukoma staminea* Native steamer often wild-harvested alongside invasive Manilas.

RAZOR CLAM *Siliqua patula* Delicious and delicate, razors require wave action. Spring brings harvesters with PVC clam guns [and licenses] to tribally co-managed coastal beaches like Mocrocks and Kalaloch.

WEATHERVANE SCALLOP *Patinopecten caurinus* Also known as the giant Pacific, weathervanes can reach 9 inches in shell diameter. Manna for chefs, mystery for scientists. ["Testy, hard to work with," laments one fisheries biologist.]

THE OLYMPIC MARMOT

The most convivial creature of Olympic National Park, the Olympic marmot [*Marmota olympus*] is also endemic to this particular alpine stretch of the Northwest, where they make a home in mountain meadows. Affectionate, deeply sociable and verbal, the list of reasons to hold these housecat-sized rodents in a certain awe is lengthy. They use a system of shrill chirps and whistles for general communication, including all-important warnings of danger or intruders. In the summer, these marmots often double their body weight by feasting on a bounty of tender shoots and flowers [like lupine and glacier lilies]. And during their cold-season hibernation, they undergo "torpor," existing on stored fat and maintaining an ambient body temperature and slow heart rate. By sumer, furry pups can be spotted venturing out of their burrows and engaging in enthusiastic play. Luckily, close to 90 percent of their habitat within the park is protected.

BIRDS OF NOTE

SOOTY GROUSE *Dendragapus fuliginosus* The male flashes color, shading from pale blue to deep gray. Look for a blaze of orange in its crown as it haunts conifer forests along Hurricane Ridge.

RHINOCEROS AUKLET *Cerorhinca monocerata* This relative of the puffin is a coast-dweller, where it forages while swimming underwater. The beak's "horn" [hence the name] grows in spring.

STELLER'S JAY *Cyanocitta stelleri* "Shook-shook" call can be heard in areas rich with pine, spruce and fir. Can also mimic the scream of a hawk.

WILLOW FLYCATCHER *Empidonax traillii* Breeds in thickets of deciduous trees, especially willows, as well as brushy fields and copses.

BELTED KINGFISHER *Megaceryle alcyon* Watch for rapid wings beating before a headfirst plunge for fish. Females boast rusty belly band.

NORTHERN FLICKER *Colaptes auratus* A sunset of color peeks from under wings and tail when this woodpecker is in flight; otherwise known for a red shaft, spotted breast and ringing call.

THE ROOSEVELT ELK

A field note on Cervus elaphus roosevelti

Olympic National Park is home to the largest herd of Roosevelt elk in the Pacific Northwest—their presence key to the national park's history. The 19th-century Olympic Forest Reserve was created, in part, to protect the elk. In 1909, Theodore Roosevelt designated part of the region as Mount Olympus National Monument, and in 1938, Franklin Roosevelt signed the act responsible for turning monument to park. Come September, the bugles, roars, whistles and barks of bulls can be heard as they compete for mates, especially in the Hoh Rain Forest. Velveteen-antlered [shed and regrown every year], dark-coated and majestic to behold, they play a vital role in a healthy park ecosystem: as the peninsula's most prolific herbivore—on average, most weigh between 600 and 700 pounds—they clear understory ferns, shrubs and lichen in the forest, making way for other flora and fauna.

PREDATORS

Black bears, cougars and gray wolves prey on adult elk and their calves [along with their more compact counterparts, deer]. Roosevelt elk have an evolutionary edge when it comes to self-defense: exceptional senses of smell and hearing that increase danger awareness, plus a speedy running pace of 35 miles per hour.

SELECT MOLES

TOWNSEND'S MOLE *Scapanus townsendii* The largest North American mole. Velvety black fur, loves moist, loamy soils.

COAST MOLE *Scapanus orarius* A true Left Coaster, ranging from California to British Columbia. Expert earthworm hunter.

SNOW MOLE *S. townsendii olympicus* Endemic variant of Townsend's, lives only here. Rare dweller of the alpine zone.

SELECTED CONTENT

MORE THAN 25 ENTRIES

Excerpts have been edited for clarity and concision.

Historical lore, characters, incidents, facts and key context that shaped Olympic and its surrounds

TREE OF LIFE

It has no official name. As many have noted, it is absent from any authoritative map of the National Park, and enjoys no particular status as far as the National Park Service is concerned. Yet in our current age, which covets natural imagery to post on main, this Sitka spruce near Kalaloch Lodge has become a coastal icon. It does make a striking sight: light-gray roots gnarled in an upside-down Medusa's mane and hanging in space, as the tree clings to opposite sides of a narrow ravine. It can't last long, everyone says, and yet for now it endures. A symbol of ecology's fragile resilience, perhaps—certainly, an oft-visited, photographed example of the Olympic seashore's brawn and delicacy. Arguably ironically, the Sitka's dramatic predicament is man-made, resulting from erosion caused by 1960s culvert construction. This mundane fact does not dull its appeal, which borders on the mystical.

COPPER CANYON PRESS

In 1972, four UC Santa Barbara graduates—fresh off a win for best college literary magazine, with $500 prize money—bought equipment to produce the first book published by Copper Canyon Press. [Early works were printed from hand-set type on antique letterpresses]. Two years later, the press found its permanent home at a military fort-turned-arts complex in Port Townsend. Since then, Copper Canyon has maintained its ardor for poetry, publishing almost 700 titles and cultivating steadfast readers. A list of beloved poets from the Copper Canyon stacks—including Nobel and National Book Award honorees:

PABLO NERUDA
CAROLYN KIZER
LUCILLE CLIFTON
JERICHO BROWN
JIM HARRISON
RABINDRANATH TAGORE
JUNE JORDAN
W.S. MERWIN

RED PINE
RUTH STONE
C.D. WRIGHT
HAYDEN CARRUTH
ARTHUR SZE
OCEAN VUONG
ODYSSEAS ELYTIS
LUCIA PERILLO

DUNGENESS CRAB

Named for the wild and forlorn Dungeness Spit,
Metacarcinus magister *shaped West Coast cuisine.*
Its meat was the preferred ingredient for this classic.

SOLARI'S CRAB LOUIS — Take meat of crab in large pieces and dress with the following: One-third mayonnaise, two-thirds chili sauce, small quantity chopped English chow-chow, a little Worcestershire sauce and minced tarragon, shallots and sweet parsley. Season with salt and pepper and keep on ice. —*Bohemian San Francisco,* 1914

OLYMPIA BEER

"BIG BUILDINGS AT TUMWATER."
The Tacoma Daily Ledger
October 5, 1896

While for several months there has been a general cessation of building operations in this city, two handsome structures have been erected over by the falls of historic Tumwater, one of the first white settlements north of the Columbia. For the past year, workmen have been busy and the site where once stood the oldest tannery in the territory has been changed completely. Leopold F. Schmidt is one of the wealthiest brewers of Montana. While visiting in Olympia last year, his attention was attracted by the superior advantages the water power at Tumwater afforded for the purposes of his business, and before he left for home he had purchased the water power and site for a brewery and ice factory. With the natural advantages of both water power and water transportation right at the door, Mr. Schmidt determined that his brewery be a modern one, and so it is. In fact it is doubtful if the whole country contains an institution with such advantages that not even a wagon is necessary in distributing the firm's output. It is all done by electricity.

Olympia Beer and the Tumwater Brewing Company were mainstays of Northwestern merriment until 2021, when no "superior advantages" could sustain the flow of suds in a changed industry.

THE MOUNTAINEERS

1864 Outdoor enthusiasts gather at the foot of Mount Hood in Oregon, with 35 women and 155 men climbing to the summit to begin mountaineering organization the Mazamas

1906 The Mazamas hold an expedition on Mount Baker in Washington, where a Seattle-based cohort forms an auxiliary organization: The Mountaineers. Founders include photographer Asahel Curtis, state geologist Henry Landes and businessman W. Montelius Price.

JAN 1907 The Mountaineers elect Landes as first president. [His wife, Bertha, would become Seattle's first female mayor in 1926.] Women make up more than half of charter members.

MAR 1907 The club produces its first log, *The Mountaineer Annual*. In the foreword, Landes calls The Mountaineers "an association of kindred spirits who love the out-of-doors and to whom the wildwood, the flowery mead and the mountain fastness afford a rest, a solace, and an inspiration."

JUL 1907 The club's first summer hike explores the Olympic Mountains and Mount Olympus

NOV 1907 "Auxiliary to the Mazamas" dropped from club name

1914 Construction finishes on the first Mountaineers lodge, a club hub near the skiing and winter sports of Snoqualmie Pass

1938 A group of 24 Mountaineers form a separate entity, the Recreational Equipment Cooperative, each paying $1 for membership dues to help acquire improved equipment. The group eventually becomes REI.

1955 A volunteer committee of Mountaineers informally gathers to create a mountaineering training text

1960 Publication of *Mountaineering: The Freedom of the Hills*, soon a perennial subcultural classic and oft-revised staple of American climbing

1971 A copy of Mountaineer Books' *The Alpine Lakes* helps persuade President Gerald Ford to sign legislation to protect a wilderness area, one of many conservation efforts by the group

2023 The Mountaineers have 15,000 active members in the Pacific Northwest; Mountaineer Books has 700 titles in print on outdoor recreation and conservation

TRIANGLE OF FIRE

At the turn of the 20th century, the "Triangle of Fire" was the main line of naval defense for the entrance to Puget Sound. Beach and bluff camouflaged mammoth shore batteries across a triad of military bases: Forts Casey, Flagler and Worden. After two world wars, the bases were decommissioned and transferred to Washington's state park system. Now, they are both spooky bunker ghost towns and bustling recreation hubs, drawing campers and beachgoers.

FORT FLAGLER Fort Flagler was the first, activated in 1899. Twenty-six artillery pieces overlooked Admiralty Inlet from the northern end of Marrowstone Island through the Korean War. Today, visitors come for the marine camping park and saltwater shoreline.

FORT CASEY The guns first fired on September 11, 1901 on Whidbey Island, and within 20 years of construction, Casey housed 10 officers and 428 enlisted men. Now, it's part of a compound of more than 100 historic structures, and the Pacific Northwest Trail slices through it.

FORT WORDEN Port Townsend's Fort Worden was home to 12-inch "disappearing" guns that each weighed more than 100,000 pounds—and had a range of more than 10 miles. Houses of officers who once scanned horizons here can now be rented.

CASTAWAYS

The tale of the so-called "Three Kichis" makes a haunting entry into the maritime lore of the North Pacific. In 1832, a powerful current seized a Japanese vessel called *Hojunmaru* and carried her far out to sea. Adrift, most of the crew died of scurvy. But in January of '34, the battered hulk washed ashore at Cape Flattery, and Makah seal hunters encountered—to their astonishment—three young men. Known as Iwakichi, Kyukichi and Otokichi, the survivors then led strange lives as pawns of international politics; they were, for example, thought to be the first Japanese people ever to visit London, though ultimately they were deposited in Macau. Only one ever saw Japan again: Otokichi, who became a well-regarded translator and changed his name to John Matthew Ottoson.

EVERGREEN STATE COLLEGE

Famous for a freewheeling approach to alternative education, this bastion of free thought has helped define Olympian culture since the late '60s.

Letter from the President, 1971

The prospective student may be attracted to Evergreen by the absence of some old familiar forms such as GPAs, set class periods, lists of courses to be taken as arbitrary hurdles. Before he considers coming to Evergreen he should think whether it is merely to escape these superficialities, and he should look beyond to the self-discipline he'll need to stick to a task that presumably he himself picked as worth doing. More to the point, he may be attracted by the magnificent opportunity for an individualized program of study. But he should recognize that he will be confronted by the realities of mind, matter, and work. Escape from these realities—ironically—can be made only at cost to one's own individuality...he should be willing to go beyond his prior notions of whatever a "standard" college might be. Evergreen is not an established college; it is an institution in process.

1971-1972 *Catalog Highlights*
CAUSALITY, FREEDOM, AND CHANCE
THE PLAY'S THE THING: THEN AND NOW
SPACE, TIME, AND FORM
CONTEMPORARY AMERICAN MINORITIES
PROBLEM SOLVING: GAMES AND PUZZLES
THE INDIVIDUAL IN AMERICA

"WASHINGTON STATE"

In 1851, settlers north of the Columbia demanded separation from vast Oregon Territory. After conventions, screeds to Congress and fiery speeches, legislative gears began to turn. The debate focused not on the need for a new territory, but its name. Some feared the proposed "Columbia" would cause confusion with the capital District of the same name. A Kentucky congressman offered, as a solution ... Washington. A degree of confusion persists to this day.

GEORGE BUSH

The particular George Bush of which the passage below speaks was a Black fur trapper and Army veteran, born in Pennsylvania in 1790. In 1845, he migrated to the Pacific Northwest with a party of settlers under one Colonel Simmons. Bush Prairie, WA bears his name.

George Bush was a colored man, a man of intelligence and great force of character, who deservedly commanded the respect of his associates and neighbors. He had left Missouri because it was a slave State. He migrated to Oregon, north of slavery's line of thirty-six degrees, thirty minutes, which he expected to find 'free territory.' Before his arrival, the color line had been drawn by the passage of the proscriptive law against his race, inhibiting people of color residing within the territory. North of the Columbia river, where, at that time, British influence controlled, the enforcement of that law was altogether improbable. Besides, it was a prevalent opinion that the Columbia river would be adopted as the boundarv line; that north of that river it would possibly continue to be British soil. George, knowing that 'slaves cannot breathe in England,' felt that, for him and his race, north of the Columbia was the preferable location. There is no doubt that George Bush was actuated by such opinions to seek a residence on the north side of the river; nor is it saying too much for the influence he exerted in that little band to claim the svmpathy of his associates with his condition, after that long march with them to escape that pro-slavery atmosphere which crushed out his humanity, had much to do in determining the Simmons colony to settle upon Puget Sound." —*History of the Pacific Northwest,* by Evan Elwood, 1889

INTERNATIONAL POP UNDERGROUND CONVENTION

An August 1991 punk festival in Olympia endures in legend as a sort of Monterey Pop Festival for the '90s underground—concluding just two days before Nirvana, product of Aberdeen and Olympia, released "Smells Like Teen Spirit." Partial roster:

BEAT HAPPENING
BIKINI KILL
FUGAZI
UNWOUND
FASTBACKS
BUILT TO SPILL
MELVINS
BRATMOBILE
KICKING GIANT
HEAVENS TO BETSY
7 YEAR BITCH
THE NATION OF ULYSSES

HARD RAIN CAFE

Store hours, as posted at the last grub stop on Upper Hoh Road.

OPEN MOST DAYS AROUND 8:00 OR 9:00 AM;
OCCASIONALLY AS EARLY AS 7:30 AM, BUT
SOME DAYS AS LATE AS 9:30 OR 10:00 AM

WE CLOSE AROUND 5:30 OR 6:00 PM
BUT SOMETIMES AS LATE AS 7:00 OR 8:00 PM

SOME DAYS OR AFTERNOONS
WE AREN'T HERE AT ALL!
AND LATELY WE'VE BEEN HERE JUST ABOUT
ALL THE TIME, EXCEPT WHEN WE'RE FISHING OR HUNTING.
BUT WE SHOULD BE HERE THEN, TOO!!

PAN ROAST OF OYSTERS

Morning Olympian, 1922

[For six persons.] Put over fire in frying-pan or kettle a slice of butter about 1-inch thick off the end of a 2-pound roll. Drain thoroughly and dry one quarter of Olympia oysters in colander and remove any particle of shell; when the butter is melted place the oysters in the butter and roast them till edges begin to curl. Have ready mixed, in separate receptacle, one teacup of best tomato catsup, three drops of tabasco sauce, one dessert spoon of old-fashioned pepper sauce, one dessert spoon of Worcestershire sauce, one teaspoonful of salt. Pour over oysters roasted in butter as above, and keep over fire until heated through. Serve hot on slices of buttered toast.

This recipe originates [allegedly] from Doane's Oyster House, an Olympia institution in the 1880s. As one historian wrote: "For a whole generation, most of the political maneuvers in Washington territory and state were devised in Doane's Oyster House over hot plates of his famous Pan Roast."

EARLY NIRVANA

1967 .... Kurt Cobain born in Aberdeen, WA, son of a waitress and a mechanic

1980s .... High school pal Roger Osborne [later, "King Buzzo" of Montesano-founded band Melvins] introduces Cobain to punk music

1985 .... Forms first band, charismatically named Fecal Matter

1987 .... First incarnation of Nirvana with bassist and fellow Melvins fan Krist Novoselic

1987-89..... Frequent shows in Olympia, Tacoma, Seattle, Aberdeen, Hoquiam, etc.

1988 .... Jan.: First recording session with producer Jack Endino: 10 songs, five hours

.... Nov.: "Love Buzz" marks the debut of subscription "Singles Club" from Seattle label Sub Pop

1989 .... Cobain moves into triplex apartments on Pear Street in Olympia. *Bleach* released.

1990 .... Dave Grohl, formerly of Washington, D.C. band Scream, joins as drummer

Ca. 1990 ... Bikini Kill singer Kathleen Hanna scrawls "KURT SMELLS LIKE TEEN SPIRIT" on Pear Street wall

1991........... April: Live debut of "Smells Like Teen Spirit" at Seattle show featuring Olympia groups Fitz of Depression and Bikini Kill

.... Aug.: Noted performance at Reading Festival in U.K.

.... Sept: Major-label album *Nevermind* released. MTV debuts "Smells Like Teen Spirit" video, directed by Samuel Bayer.

.... Oct: *Nevermind* certified gold

The wider region's music heritage includes performers such as Anacortes-rooted Phil Elverum and Karl Blau; acclaimed bands such as Sleater-Kinney [named for an Olympia thoroughfare]; and respected record labels K and Kill Rock Stars. The **RIOT GRRRL** *movement—strongly linked to Olympia musicians—became internationally influential in the early* 1990*s.*

MARINE MAMMALS

NORTHERN SEA OTTER *Enhydra lutris kenyoni*
Weighing between 50 to 100 pounds, these furry aquatic creatures make "rafts" of kelp to float upon in packs while resting and eating.

PACIFIC HARBOR SEAL *Phoca vitulina richardii*
Gray, spotted bodies are wrapped in blubber for warmth. Whiskered faces. Known for "galumphing."

ORCA *Orcinus orca*
Technically the largest dolphin species, this distinctive apex predator, with white markings on black body, will eat any fish, as well as seabirds.

GRAY ORT WORDLE *Eschrichtius robustus*
Stirs up clouds of nutrients from ocean floor, nourishing other creatures. Babies are whoppers: up to 2,000 pounds.

HUMPBACK WHALE *Megaptera novaeangliae*
While not an apex predator, individuals still consume up to 3,000 pounds of food per day. Humps surface as they breathe—keep an eye out.

OLYMPUS MANOR

The Pacific Northwest's countercultural bent no doubt runs deep—something to do, perhaps, with freebooting trappers, sailors and timberjacks encountering Indigenous and Asian influences in a dynamic, demanding environment. [It's a theory.] But a thread can be traced to a curious establishment on Hood Canal: Olympus Manor. This outpost in tiny Union was built in the early 1920s, with Orientalist motifs and art deco style. The Manor attracted a creative scene that orbited around Tacoma high school art teacher and committed bohemian Orré Nobles. The influential woodblock artist Waldo Spore Chase, maker of misty and poetic images indebted to Japanese aesthetics and the Arts & Crafts Movement, was likewise prominent. For three decades, the Manor hosted gatherings of music and art lovers that hinted at the Beat and hippie upheavals to come. Though the structure burned in 1952, its legacy can still be detected in pockets of independent thought and culture that thrive around the region.

FUGITIVE

The Spokane Press, April 8, 1912

DEADLY RIFLE OF SUPPOSED MANIAC WREAKS HAVOC WITH MAN HUNTERS

First of all, try to picture John Tornow, the beast-man. Your mental picture should be of dead-black eyes glowing through lids narrowed to slits. From them shines a hate insensate of all humankind. In his hate he has slain six men, if accounts be true, in cold blood. Two were of his own blood—his sister's sons. Two were strangers whom he slew for gain. And two were deputies who had dared to match their forest cunning against the matchless cunning of the beast-man. The beast-man's cheeks are thin, his cheek-bones high, his nose aquiline. He stands well over six feet in his moccasins, and his shoulders are broad and his chest deep. His loins are as slim, comparatively, as a greyhound's, and when he moves, it is with the swift stealthiness of the panther. Picture him now moving through the forest gloom. He gropes rather than walks, with a long, swinging, distance-killing stride, and never a twig snaps or leaf rustles to herald his progress. He is hatless, and his black hair hangs in dark locks over his shoulders. A rifle rests in the crook of his arm.

"The Wild Man of the Wynoochee," Turnow was done in by a posse out of Montesano in 1913. *He remains a figure of lore.*

MURDER CASE

The national park's idyllic vistas stood in dreadful contrast to one grim historical moment: the so-called Lady of the Lake case of 1940, when the blanket-wrapped body of Hallie Latham Illingworth surfaced in Lake Crescent's tranquil waters. Some horrid natural process had transformed her flesh into a soap-like substance—this is called "saponification," they say. The discovery became a regional sensation, ending in a 1942 trial, avidly followed by a populace seeking distraction from World War II, and the second-degree murder conviction of Illingworth's husband Monty. [In his mugshot: a creepily grinning smalltown Lothario.] He served nine years.

LOGGING VOCABULARY

"When you are able to 'punch' a donkey, 'buck' 2000 feet of straw-line and 'hang' a block you'll be a man, my son, for a' of that. To the untutored brain, punching a donkey might seem like a ticklish occupation. However, once you have discovered that the donkey is not one of the long-eared variety, the situation becomes less involved. The much-cussed species of steam engine known to the profession as a 'donkey' is to the logging game as the mainspring is to your dollar watch. It's the source of power that makes the wheels of industry go 'round and 'round." *—How to Become a Logger: A Complete Treatise in Six Lessons* by D.D. Strite [1924]

COAST SALISH GAMBLING GAMES

For thousands of years, the first peoples of the Olympic Peninsula have made a rich life from salmon and cedar, sea and mountains. Like now, tribal groups of the past may not have shared a common language or world view. But it's likely that they shared in the Coast Salish gambling games still played today. *Slahal,* sometimes called bone or stick games, come in at least three forms: dice, disc and hand. In many, the basic tools are intricately carved sets made from materials like yew, ivory, and beaver teeth, either thrown or hidden inside hands, prompting opponents to hazard guesses. Players play for stakes. Traditionally, these could include anything from food and clothes to houses, slaves, and guns. [An anthropologist working with the Quileute Tribe said wagering could get so wild that "there had to be a rule against a man's betting his wife and children."] Today, serious prize money can be on the line. Slahal games can be raucous, accompanied by heckling, sleight of hand and an entire ouvre of music. Oral records and secondary sources indicate that dice was a game for women, with some thrown objects gendered [and cheating part of the attraction]. Disc games brought still higher stakes, often testing leaders—and potentially their social standing. But the Hand Game [sometimes referred to as the "bloodless war"] is next level—and the most popular now. It's a team sport, with opposing sides equipped with giant tally sticks and concealable marked bones. According to some, the hand game was part of the fabric of winter village communities. Today, summer festivalgoers play the hand game for hours, drawing big crowds at celebrations like Makah Days and the Lummi Nation Stommish Water Festival.

RAYMOND CARVER

Born in Clatskanie, OR in 1938, and raised in Yakima, WA, Raymond Carver became a short-story writer and poet deeply associated with a working-class Northwest aesthetic. His minimalist sentences and hard-bitten milieu profoundly influenced American fiction in the 1970s and '80s, and still reverberates in the region's writing. Late in a career marked by both celebrated publications and notorious bouts of alcohol abuse, Carver sobered up and settled in Port Angeles with wife and fellow writer Tess Gallagher. He died there, from lung cancer, in 1988, just three months after the publication of Pulitzer-finalist collection *Where I'm Calling From*. His grave in Olympic View Cemetery remains a literary pilgrimage site. Three glimpses of Carver's trademark style and atmosphere:

A man without hands came to the door to sell me a photograph of my house. Except for the chrome hooks, he was an ordinary-looking man of fifty or so.

"How did you lose your hands?" I asked after he'd said what he wanted.

"That's another story," he said. "You want this picture or not?"

"Come in," I said. "I just made coffee."

— **"VIEWFINDER," 1978**

The people who were better than us were comfortable.
They lived in painted houses with flush toilets.
Drove cars whose year and make were recognizable.
Those worse off were sorry and didn't work.
Their strange cars sat on blocks in dusty yards.

— **"SHIFTLESS," 1985**

I was out of work. But any day I expected to hear from up north. I lay on the sofa and listened to the rain. Now and then I'd lift up and look through the curtain for the mailman.

There was no one on the street, nothing.

I hadn't been down again five minutes when I heard someone walk onto the porch, wait, and then knock. I lay still. I knew it wasn't the mailman. I knew his steps. You can't be too careful if you're out of work and you get notices in the mail or else pushed under your door. They come around wanting to talk, too, especially if you don't have a telephone.

—**"COLLECTORS," 1975**

BEACHES

From *My Wilderness: The Pacific West*
William O. Douglas, 1960

Each headland presents a beach of distinction. Some have sand made from dark volcanic rock, and packed so hard that a deer leaves few tracks on it. Some beaches are filled with a whitish, loose sand that flows freely between the toes. Others have sand, too coarse for packing, that is streaked with pebbles. Some of this sand is so loose and heavy that half of every step is lost in backward movement. And few are a millennium from hard-packed sand, being lined with boulders and ledges of rock that tides without number have yet to pulverize. Most beaches have logs strewn along them or piled high on their upper reaches. Some of them have fallen from the adjoining forest, worked loose by the angry tides that come with winter gales and bite ferociously into the land. Some logs have broken loose from booms pulled by tugs far out beyond the dangerous shoals. Logs that reach the beach in the winter have been rolled smooth by summer. Some giants have been piled so high by ferocious waves as to be dozens of feet beyond the reach of any high tide that comes in September.

Pieces of ships, wrecked on hidden reefs, are often added to the pile. Once Augie and I came across a fishing vessel quite intact and sitting upright in the sand as if in drydock for repairs. And it is on these Olympic beaches that one can find the prized Japanese glass balls that have broken away from the fishing nets they help float and drifted thousands of miles across the Pacific. I have found so many I had no room to carry them.

The force of winds and tides is often so great as to change completely the character of some beaches from one year to the next. On my first hike Augie and I stopped for lunch on a beach of hard sand where a clear, cold stream came tumbling out of the forest on to the white beach. ... The beach was almost as hard as concrete, and this smooth sand extended even beyond the limits of low tide.

William O. Douglas [1898-1980] *was the longest serving U.S. Supreme Court justice ever. He wrote eloquent travel memoirs, and often sojourned in the Northwest, e.g., meeting a wife* [*one of several*] *at Mount Saint Helens.*

HISTORIC STRUCTURES

STORM KING RANGER STATION Contradictory reports say 1905 or 1909 for this sturdy little cabin. Either way, it could be the oldest surviving structure in the Lake Crescent area.

SOL DUC HOT SPRINGS RESORT A grand old-time water-cure palace: 165 rooms, a sanatorium, golf and croquet, all ranged around the healing, sulfurous waters of Sol Duc. Opened in 1912. Just four years later, a fire destroyed the building. Never restored to its original grandeur.

CANYON CREEK SHELTER In the 1930s, the Civilian Conservation Corps unit at Camp Elwha built a series of forest shelters. This is the last one standing, with a pair of dignified pillars supporting a cupola.

HURRICANE RIDGE DAY LODGE Another tale of fire and woe. Built in 1952 in the midst of the national parks' postwar visitation boom, this was the jump-off point for summer hiking and winter ski adventures. In May 2023, with an $11-million remodel ongoing, a fire consumed the structure, leaving only charred foundation.

HUMES RANCH CABIN An Elwha River homestead, once used as a filming base for a Disney documentary on the region's elk. Keep hiking to reach dramatic Dodger Point Bridge.

BOTTEN CABIN Another Elwha outpost, one of the last remaining old hunting camps in the park's backcountry. Noted for the excellence of its hand-built construction.

ENCHANTED VALLEY CHALET An imposing, block-like refuge, deep in the Quinault Rain Forest, its hand-hewn, silver-fir walls were first erected in 1931, far from the nearest road, as a lodge for weary hikers. Now long closed, the two-story structure hits a somewhat ghostly note, sitting precariously on eroding riverbank even after its 2014 move.

LOW DIVIDE BATHHOUSE A remnant of a remnant. Along with Enchanted Valley, a throwback to pre-national-park days of private companies building forest lodgings. Now the last piece of a bygone chalet.

REI

1935..... Seattle adventurers Lloyd and Mary Anderson dislike local gear purveyors; they order an Akadem Pickel ice axe from Austria instead. Cost: $3.50, postage included.

1938..... The Andersons open REI—a co-op—in Seattle, selling quality climbing gear to friends and other outdoor enthusiasts.

1944..... The co-op sets up camp in downtown Seattle at 523 Pike Street.

1945..... Legendary gear rental program launched.

1963..... Grand opening of main Seattle digs at 1525 11th Avenue.

1963..... First full-time employee, Jim Whittaker, is first American to summit Mount Everest.

1970..... Nearly 200,000 members, two retail stores and more than $5 million in annual sales. Lloyd Anderson retires as manager and CEO.

1975..... Crowds flock to the grand opening of REI's Berkeley, California store.

1977..... The inaugural Twinkie Roast tradition, a fervent plea for snow, takes place.

1980..... 1 million members, six retail stores and $50 million in annual sales.

1988..... Co-op starts an in-house, six-person product development team

1993..... When three Seattle employees die on Mount Rainier, REI creates the REI Memorial Fund [later, the REI Foundation].

1994..... Ranked as the sixth largest sports apparel retailer in the United States.

1996..... A new flagship store in Seattle opens; REI.com launches as the largest outdoor gear shop on the Internet.

2000..... Sally Jewell made CEO; in 2013, she will be nominated for U.S. Secretary of the Interior.

2002..... The Half Dome—priced at $149—is the first two-door, two-vestibule, two-person tent.

2013..... Return policy changed from a lifetime guarantee to 365-day return window.

2015..... On Black Friday, web sales and all stores close, giving employees a paid day off.

2017..... Co-founder Mary Anderson dies at 107.

2020..... REI pledges to halve its carbon footprint by 2030.

FISHING CONTROVERSY

"I live here. I fish here!" According to legend, a teenaged Billy Frank Jr., shouted these words at Washington State game wardens in 1945, just before his violent arrest on the banks of the Nisqually River. Frank, a citizen of the Nisqually Tribe, knew the Medicine Creek Treaty of 1854 entitled him to fish in "all usual and accustomed" places—language mirrored in treaties signed by 20 other Western Washington tribes. Yet by the middle of the 20th century, the tribes had seen promises broken to benefit canneries and commercial fleets, facilitate land grabs and promote other forms of profiteering and control. Enter the "fish-ins" of the 1960s: defiant off-reservation acts of fishing by Frank and others intended to draw police crackdowns and media attention. [Marlon Brando, anchorman Charles Kuralt, Black Panther Billy Jackson and others made cameos.] To quell the chaos, the state sued seven treaty tribes in 1973. But Judge George Boldt instead ruled for the tribes, affirming their perpetual right to keep half of the fish passing through traditional tribal fishing grounds, regardless of reservation boundaries. For the next 40 years, Frank watched his people restore a way of life. The Boldt Decision remade fishing in Washington State, at a time when the dream of greater tribal sovereignty felt otherwise elusive. "That judge listened to all of us," Frank later said. "He let us tell our stories, right there in federal court. He made a decision, he interpreted the treaty, and he gave us a tool to help save the salmon."

RESTORING THE ELWHA

Beginning in 2011, a dam removal project reputed to be the world's largest unleashed the free flow of the Elwha River, which begins at a snowfinger high in the mountains and travels 45 miles to the Strait of Juan de Fuca. In fact, two major dams came down, after a century of blocking once-legendary salmon runs. Since the project's completion in 2014, scientific observation suggests fish populations are rebounding. In 2023, the Lower Elwha Klallam Tribe was able to resume limited ceremonial and subsistence coho fishing. Sediment freed by dam removal has also changed the estuarine ecosystem, benefiting Dungeness crab and other species.

INDIGENOUS ART

Take away the modern-day border between the United States and Canada, and give a standard north-south map a quarter turn. In this view, the Olympic Peninsula sits in the heart of a watery, ocean-bounded region of islands, sounds, rivers and inlets that stretches from the Columbia over into Alaska. This territory is home to an exceptionally complex and diverse array of Indigenous peoples, dense with different languages, traditional lifeways and political concerns. The spectrum of art runs just as wide. Even so, "Northwest Native art" has become a globally recognizable style: sharp, elegantly curving lines, bold graphic forms, motifs rooted in the natural world. No brief primer could encompass either the historic or contemporary creativity of the region, but here are some starting points:

WELCOME FIGURES Huge carved human forms traditionally stood watch over beaches and other points of contact. In recent years, prominent new installations have revived awareness of the tradition and symbolize ancestral ties between particular tribes and their territories. Notable examples can be seen at the Makah Cultural and Resource Center in Neah Bay; the Waterfront Center in Edmonds; and on Tacoma's Prairie Line Trail.

TOTEM POLES Totem poles are *not* traditional to the Olympic Peninsula or Puget Sound-area tribes. They originate further north, with peoples living in present-day Canada and Alaska. They became popularly associated with the U.S. Pacific Northwest starting in 1899, when some Seattle businessmen blatantly stole a Tlingit pole in Alaska and installed it in the city center as a promotional device. That vexed history has gotten a twist in more recent times, notably through the Jamestown S'klallam Tribe's House of Myths Carving Shed. Artists working there [both Native and non-Native] have created a large number of vibrant modern poles that have served the tribe well as visual and cultural brand icons. See them at the tribe's headquarters in Sequim, the Port Townsend waterfront and elsewhere.

TRIBAL MUSEUM
Suquamish Museum
Suquamish
Traditional longhouse, grave of Si'ahl [Chief Seattle].

MAJOR COLLECTION
Burke Museum
Seattle
Weavings, carvings, masks: more than 11,000 items.

BOOK
Where the Power Is: Indigenous Perspectives on Northwest Coast Art
[Duffek, McLennan and Wilson, 2021.]

"THE PROPOSED OLYMPIC NATIONAL PARK"

In the early part of the 20th century, conservationists—notably Rosalie Barrow Edge and Willard Van Name—argued that the Olympic Peninsula required urgent protection. This 1934 manifesto influenced Congress and President Roosevelt in the National Park's creation.

THE LAST CHANCE FOR A MAGNIFICENT AND UNIQUE NATIONAL PARK

The completion, several years ago, of a motor highway entirely around the Olympic Peninsula, Washington, often called "our last frontier," which contains one of the largest unsettled areas left in the United States excluding Alaska, has brought about a crisis in the history of the region, and makes it imperative to act promptly if we are to save any considerable part of its magnificent forests from annihilation and its wildlife from extinction.

IMPORTANCE AS A BIG GAME REFUGE

For preserving the game animals of that part of the country this Peninsula affords an ideal place. In its central and western parts the Roosevelt elk, the largest and finest variety of the elk, still survives in some numbers, and this region affords the only practicable place [in United States territory at least] where there is any hope of permanently preserving this magnificent animal. There do not seem to be any reasons why, with adequate protection from their human enemies, the moose, mountain sheep, and mountain goat might not be permanently established there.

THE OLYMPIC PENINSULA FORESTS

These are, however, by no means the only, and not really the most important and urgent reasons for protecting the area. The Peninsula affords the last opportunity for preserving any adequately large remnants of the wonderful primeval forests of Douglas fir, hemlock, cedar, and spruce which were not so many years ago one of the grandest and the most unique features of our two northwesternmost States, but which everywhere have been or are being logged off to the very last stick. Soon hardly an acre of such forests will remain anywhere to show what they were like .... It is too late to save any of the finest stands of this timber—they are all gone already, and will take six centuries at least to grow again—but the best tract that we can still save is in the Olympic Peninsula.

INCLUDING

An exploration of the national park's attractions and activities—plus 10 strategic base camps

THE NORTH

The park's most prominent gateway makes a passage of transformation, with the route inbound ascending quickly from the hard-working streets of Port Angeles into loftier, mistier, greener realms. Even the short jaunt to Lake Crescent shifts perspectives, glimmering waters sprawling between dramatic mountain rises, the forest gathering all around as a gentle but palpable silence. A big wild lies beyond the end of the road.

HISTORY

Rosemary Inn

Lodge built 1915, now non-profit NatureBridge's HQ

CAMP

Fairholme

Scores of sites at lake's edge. Angle for C Loop.

NATURE

Beardslee trout

Unique rainbow variety, found only in Crescent.

HIKING TRAILS

SPRUCE RAILROAD TRAIL

Four mellow miles along the lake, a good call for young ramblers. Traces of rail and industry abound. A memorable bridge spans lake waters, and small rises command azure views.

PYRAMID PEAK

About 6.5 miles out and back, a vigorous parallel to the Crescent shore. Vaults nearly 2,500 feet to a mountaintop view. Hiking poles recommended, washouts sometimes reported. Check first.

MINK LAKE

Leaving from Sol Duc Resort: five miles, round trip, reaches a tiny lake via a collage of forest stages [second growth, then old growth] and a spring/summer wildflower spectrum.

BACKCOUNTRY

With no roads traversing the park, Olympic is made for wide-ranging adventure. All overnight or multiday expeditions into the backcountry require permits, obtained via recreation.gov. [On less than seven days' notice, call the Wilderness Information Center: 360-565-3100.] Certain areas—including **SOL DUC** and the Seven Lakes Basin, the country beyond road's end at the **OBSTRUCTION POINT TRAILHEAD**, and others—are subject to permit quotas. Summer reservations for those areas "go live" on April 15 each year. With over 600 miles of trail in the park, routes and destinations can be the subject of infinite study. Notable backcountry domains include **THE HIGH DIVIDE**, a ridge-tracing route in the Sol Duc region that commands gemlike lake views while exploring a fertile subalpine environment; **ROARING WINDS**, a campsite peering into the Buckhorn Wilderness, deep in marmot country. Bear canisters are often required, always a decent idea.

The national park contains 130 miles of the **PACIFIC NORTHWEST TRAIL**, *designated in 2009: the climactic stretch for hikers navigating this 600-plus-mile wilderness trail from east to west. The most typical thru-hike route begins in Montana's Glacier National Park in July, aiming to reach the Olympic coast by September. The trail is recognized as the legacy of backcountry legend* **RON STRICKLAND**, *whose 2011 memoir,* Pathfinder, *tells the tale.*

HURRICANE RIDGE

SUMMER Just 17 miles from Port Angeles, Hurricane Ridge is one of the northern park's iconic destinations. Known among day-trippers for its sweep of mountain views and high-alpine atmosphere, it is also take-off point for a number of trails, including hikes to Klahhane Ridge and Elwha Ranger Station.

WINTER As the name suggests, the ridge sees ferocious winter storms and snowfall, fostering one of few lift-operating ski areas within the national parks. The downhill season is a low-key, family-scale affair under the auspices of the nonprofit Hurricane Ridge Winter Sports Education Association. Nordic and snowshoe routes weave through.

HISTORY

VINTAGE LODGES

LAKE CRESCENT LODGE

Among classic national park lodges, Lake Crescent stands out not for architectural pedigree but for the quirk and texture of its history. Originally called "Singer's Lake Crescent Tavern," the shoreside compound dates to 1915. A second generation of family owners, the Bovees, expanded and revised the various cabins clustered around the throwback main lodge. The National Park Service took ownership in the 1950s; the Bovee tenure is commemorated by the nearby meadow, a light and pleasant encounter with the Olympic woods.

LOG CABIN RESORT

"The fisherman is king at Lake Crescent . . . The mere guest who comes to breathe the fresh air, walk among the pines, feast lazily on the kaleidoscopic scenery, or perchance peevishly await the arrival of the meal hour, must expect to hear fish-talk at all hours, and not feel hurt if he shall take his dinner alone, while the balance of the late-arriving and fish-smelling guests sit down in ravenous exhilaration at 10 o'clock p.m." —*Overland Magazine*, in a report from the earliest incarnation ["Log Cabin Hotel"], 1903

FDR ON TOUR

On October 1, 1937, the *Tacoma News-Tribune* reported on the president of the United States, looping his way around the Olympic Peninsula. "The tiny communities in the Olympics turned out in full force," the front-page story read. "The wooden sidewalks were jammed with men and women, many of whom had come from deep in the wilderness to glimpse the man who sits in the White House. ... The smiling chief executive beamed on the loggers, trappers, fishermen, farmers, merchants as the caravan sped on its 231-mile journey to Tacoma." Franklin Roosevelt's Northwest swing saw 100,000 flock to Seattle's streets; in Olympia, an all-call went out to Boy Scouts to assist. At Lake Crescent Lodge, FDR huddled with local big-wigs to discuss the national park proposed for the peninsula's wild core. The great New Dealer signed legislation creating the national park the next year.

SUMMIT NOTES

MOUNT ANGELES Accessed from Hurricane Ridge via the High Divide Trail, noted for its views and tough scrambling. Some sections to the summit are categorized as Class 3 climbing terrain, denoting some degree of technical challenge. Four miles, trailhead to summit.

MOUNT MYSTERY A trek into the woods south of Sequim [and down Forest Road 2870] leads to the Upper Dungeness Trail. A three-day jaunt from there can attain one of the Olympics' five highest summits, including a view of Mystery Glacier.

MOUNT TOWNSEND One of the park's most popular alpine destinations, with four trails to the top and a rotation of seasonal attractions, from spring wildflowers to summer berries to fall colors. The commonly used 8-mile roundtrip launches from "upper" Mount Townsend trailhead, reached via road [FS-2700190].

ACTIVITIES

SOL DUC HOT SPRINGS

Sitting in a picturesque valley carved out by the Sol Duc River, Sol Duc Hot Springs Resort is rustic-ish collection of cabins and pools, open spring to fall. The main attraction: three hot mineral pools. After a long hike [or even a short one], soak in 100-degree water, taking in the surrounding towering evergreens. The suites and cabins here don't overflow with personality, but they're clean and modern; if not staying, purchase a day pass for the healing hot pools. The backstory is as interesting as the present scene: timber baron Michael Earles opened a lavish resort in this remote spot in 1912. He claimed the springs had cured a serious illness of his, and spent over half a million dollars on the resort, described as a "mecca for the sick, careworn, [the] pleasure-seeker and the sportsman." The grounds included a sanatorium, bathhouse, and croquet grounds, among other things. Just four years after its completion, a disastrous fire burned most of the resort to the ground. Legend has it that due to a short circuit, Beethoven's "Funeral March" played repeatedly on the organ while the resort went up in flames.

BIKING TO OLYMPIC HOT SPRINGS

When the Elwha Dam was removed in 2011, the river washed out the road to the trailhead for these hot springs. Now, park at Madison Falls Trailhead and bike up the old asphalt road to the original parking lot, crossing the river on your way. At the old lot—Boulder Creek Trailhead—park your bike, and set out on foot for the last two miles. Be warned: the road to the trailhead is steep, reaching gradients of 10 or 12 percent. But the trek is worth it for a dip into the unmaintained natural hot waters of Olympic Hot Springs. Rent rides at Port Townsend's The Broken Spoke.

FISHING

An abundance of lakes and rivers create a fisherman's haven for trout and salmon —the Sol Duc River and Lake Crescent are favorites. Waters West in Port Angeles will tell you what you need to know.

KAYAKING

Glide through Lake Crescent's crystalline waters. Or if salt water is more your thing, paddle along seals in the Strait of Juan de Fuca—just north of the park. Elevate Outdoors leads guided trips for both.

HOOD CANAL & THE EAST

This is, perhaps, the peninsula's most unheralded but most untamed edge, as wilderness zones stack between a shimmering fjord and the national park boundary. Rivers tumble through fern-garlanded woods. Trails lead up to waterfall views and lesser-used park portals, unlocking mountain expeditions and unending quiet. Lower down and more tightly woven to civilization, vital small towns sit at a Northwest historical crossroads.

HISTORY

Elk Lick Lodge
Deep-woods cabin, built as a fishing retreat in 1926.

CAMP

Hamma Hamma Cabin
Historic 1930s abode sleeps six; keep a sharp eye for openings.

NATURE

Bigg's killer whales
Transient orcas, lately sighted more frequently in Hood Canal.

HIKING TRAILS

NORTH FORK SKOKOMISH

A 15-mile [inbound] wander from Staircase Campground crosses into the park and ascends through valleys into alpine terrain. One highlight: mountainous views from First Divide, a big-hitter dayhike.

BIG CREEK LOOP

A family-friendly circuit on national forest land. Almost 5 miles all-in. Swoops through a forest and creeks with a half-dozen bridge crossings. Go on to the more challenging Mount Elinor trail.

NOTCH PASS

A CCC project in the 1930s, revived in the 2000s; beloved for its cool log bridge, mossy switchbacks, strenuous ascending and connections to a broader backcountry trail network. Almost 9 miles, out and back.

EXPLORATION

WILDERNESS AREAS

BUCKHORN WILDERNESS

The largest of five wilderness areas along the national park's eastern boundary. Hike Marmot Pass—an 11.5-mile out-and-back trek. The view repays 3,500 feet of elevation gain. If you're up for it, turn it into an overnight and summit Buckhorn Mountain. Don't forget to check out Tubal Cain mine—an abandoned copper mine.

THE BROTHERS WILDERNESS

The Duckabush River splits the mostly precipitous area, named after the pair of homonymous peaks. Fun fact: each peak sports its own name—Edward [south] and Arthur [north]—after the real-life Fauntleroy brothers. Summiting the double peaks should be left to experienced adventurers.

MOUNT SKOKOMISH WILDERNESS

Two rocky ridges mark the wilderness. Sawtooth Ridge—a must-hit rock climbing spot—lies on the northern ridge. The southern ridge holds a noted summit: Mount Rose. Reward yourself on the way down with a dip in Lake Cushman. The Hamma Hamma River flows in the basin between the ridges.

WONDER MOUNTAIN WILDERNESS

At only 2,349 acres, one of the smallest wildernesses in the Western U.S. A rugged adventurer's dream—there are no designated trails. With a high chance of finding true solitude, don't forget to bring a map and compass.

COLONEL BOB WILDERNESS

Named after Civil War political leader Robert Green Ingersoll. Summit the namesake peak for unrivaled 360-degree views of Lake Quinault and the Olympic Peninsula. Filled with switchbacks, it's a 7-mile hike to the top via the Colonel Bob Trail.

As of 2024, *a proposed* 126,500-*acre addition to Olympic wilderness is wending its way through Congress. See* wildolympics.org.

HISTORY

SKOKOMISH TRIBE

The southern end of Hood Canal is anchored by the 8-square-mile reservation of the **SKOKOMISH INDIAN TRIBE**, a modern sovereign nation with roots in the surrounding region. Most of the tribe's citizens identify as **TWANA**, historically the name of Salishan peoples living on and around Hood Canal; "Skokomish" is an anglicization of the Twana word *sqʷuqʷóbəš*, meaning "big river people." Along with S'Klallam and Chinacum leaders, Skokomish representatives signed the 1855 Treaty of Point No Point, ceding land under immense political pressure. [About 120 years later, the Skokomish were also party to the lawsuit that yielded the historic Boldt Decision, affirming the fishing rights of many regional Treaty Tribes.] Today, the resulting reservation territory is an economic and cultural base for about 800 enrolled tribal members. In 2017, the tribe inaugurated a striking community center designed by 7 Directions Architects, an Indigenous-owned Seattle firm, evoking traditional cedar dwellings with net-zero energy use ambitions. The tribe participates in the regular **CANOE JOURNEY** linking a number of Puget Sound-area tribal nations and publishes an excellent monthly newspaper, *The Sounder*.

ENVIRONMENTAL CHANGE

SUMMER-RUN CHUM
Seven salmonids live in Hood Canal, including a unique population of summer-run chum. After massive declines into the 1990s, improved hatchery management and restoration efforts boosted spawning numbers. The count can vary wildly year-on-year, but recent seasons have been robust enough that some believe Hood Canal's summer-run chum could be removed from the Endangered Species List—a first for a salmonid.

LAKE CUSHMAN
This 4,000-acre freshwater sliver on the Skokomish bears historical resemblance to Hetch Hetchy, Yosemite's more famous [notorious?] reservoir. In 1899, the Antlers Hotel went up on the original lake's shoreline, a destination for Theodore Roosevelt and other woodsy adventurers of the era. But dam construction, begun in 1924 to supply power to Tacoma, inundated the lodge. The site, now 150 feet deep, attracts divers and filmmakers.

THE WILD COAST

If you are here, you are *out there*, exploring one of the most remote and rugged stretches of the U.S. West Coast, a stretch of moody beaches, iconic haystack rocks, restless surf and highway stretches both woodsy and sunstruck. It can feel out of time. That is an illusion—deep history and living culture lace these shores with stories, weaving land, seascape and dynamic change.

HISTORY
Welcome Figures
Monumental carved human forms: traditional tribal symbols.

CAMP
South Beach
Stake your site within a hearty rock-toss of the breakers.

NATURE
Sea otters
Charismatic kelp floaters, much bigger than river cousins.

HIKING TRAILS

ERICSON'S BAY PRIMITIVE TRAIL

Challenging and lesser-traveled, 11 miles explore dense ancient forest, zigzagging across the spit of land that divides Ozette Lake from the sea. Connect to the South Sand Point Trail.

THIRD BEACH TRAIL

Near La Push, traverse coastal rainforest, then drop 200 feet to the beach and enter a driftwood labyrinth. To the south, spy the sea stacks and tiny isles of the Giants Graveyard.

SOUTH COAST WILDERNESS TRAIL

A potential epic, tracing beaches and timed to tides, up and down for a total of more than 2,000 feet of gain over 17 miles. Toleak Point makes a picturesque bivouac. Study the tides.

EXPLORATION

A COASTAL HIKING PRIMER

Beach hiking is a distinct pursuit. Whether out for a few hours or a whole week, consider these practical and philosophical points.

TIDES Carry a tide chart—make sure you know how to read it—as well as a detailed topographic map that notes where tides may present an issue [for instance, a headland impassable at high tide].

FOOD All food, garbage, and scented items must be stored in bear canisters [raccoons easily break into bags hung from trees].

FIRE Gather only driftwood—do not gather wood from the forest—and build fires only on the beach, at least 10 feet from beach logs.

PACE Beach hiking can have you sinking into soft sand, clambering over boulders, balancing on unstable driftwood, slipping over slick algae-covered rocks. Headland trails can be steep and muddy, and may require the use of cable ladders or fixed ropes to climb. [Bring gloves.] Take your time, and adjust your mileage goals accordingly.

OUTLOOK This is one of the most rugged stretches of coastline in the world. Pack binoculars, spend a few hours peering into the tiny universes that are tidepools and marvel at the power of the Pacific.

COASTAL POINTS OF INTEREST

NORWEGIAN MEMORIAL An austere granite obelisk amid sea stacks and coastal forest pays tribute to Norwegian sailors lost in a 1903 wreck. A mile hike in from the road, or a stop on longer north-south routes.

OIL CITY Once a focal point of petro-speculation and real estate scams, a remote outpost on the Hoh has become a small pocket of off-the-grid living. A 1.5-mile forest jaunt reaches the ocean shore.

CHILEAN MEMORIAL About a two-hour hike [rigorous] from Rialto Beach, a picturesque redoubt of sea stacks and campsites hides a plaque noting 1920 loss of the *W.J. Pirrie*, Chilean schooner.

EXPLORATION

CAPE FLATTERY

At the northwesternmost tip of the contiguous United States, a variety of forces conspire to create one of the richest environments for marine life on the Pacific coast. Well before non-Natives arrived, this was a critical spot for economic and social exchange—and a site of recurring violent conflict. It made a relatively early appearance in European records, named by Captain James Cook in 1778, just a year before his demise in Hawai'i. Today, Flattery is part of the Makah Reservation, and boardwalks carry visitors on an easy out-and-back hike [1.5 miles total] to several observation decks overlooking dramatic sandstone cliffs, wind-whipped conifers, pounding surf and deep coves. The final viewing platform faces Tatoosh Island, which was a Makah summer village for halibut fishing and whale hunting, and where a decommissioned lighthouse still stands. Bring binoculars: the rock just to the east of Tatoosh often plays home to dozens of lounging sea lions, and you can spot whales and sea otters here too.

OZETTE TRIANGLE LOOP

For some of the park's most rugged coastline, set out from the ranger station at Ozette Lake [at 8 miles long and 3 miles wide, Ozette is Washington's third largest—and largest unaltered—lake]. The 3-mile trail to **CAPE ALAVA** consists largely of lovely cedar boardwalk through dense temperate rainforest, passing at one point through a prairie where Makah people foraged for berries, dug medicinal and edible roots and hunted deer. The trail emerges onto a rocky shore. Despite the hike's popularity, there's an undeniable feeling of remoteness here, as far west as you can go in these continental United States. Spend time among the tidepools, or try to glimpse sea otters at play in the kelp beds. Continue south along the beach for another 3 miles to **SAND POINT**—about midway, look for dozens of petroglyphs at unmarked Wedding Rocks—before turning back into the forest to return to the ranger station. The full loop is about 9 miles.

CULTURE

THE OZETTE DIG & MAKAH MUSEUM

Sometimes shorthanded as "America's Pompeii"—buried in mud rather than ash—the Ozette archaeological site became one of the most significant digs ever on this continent. In 1970, a winter storm caused the sea bank just north of Cape Alava to slump, revealing well-preserved fish hooks, parts of inlaid boxes, even a canoe paddle. An 11-year excavation—a collaboration between Washington State University and the Makah Tribe—followed, producing more than 55,000 artifacts dating as far back as 2,000 years, from numerous cedar-plank longhouses. The dig gave credence to Makah oral history of a mudflow, while also providing tangible evidence of the tribe's whaling practices, woodworking and basketry skills, and architectural techniques. The findings are held at the **MAKAH CULTURAL & RESEARCH CENTER** in Neah Bay, where an excellent museum displays artifacts as well as full-sized replicas of canoes and a longhouse.

In 1999, *the Makah Tribe held its first whale hunt since the* 1920s, *the result of a complex and ongoing process around tribal rights enshrined in the* 1855 *Treaty of Neah Bay. One non-tribal account can be found in Robert Sullivan's* A Whale Hunt [2000].

CULTURE

QUILEUTE LANGUAGE

Many languages are spoken on the Peninsula. Some have been lost, including the Chimakuan language spoken by the Chimakum people until the 1940s. Chimakuan is a language group unrelated to any other known. Today, its last keepers are the Quileute and Hoh tribes. The Quileute language is one of only five on the planet without "m" and "n" sounds. It does have 12 different "k" sounds, and many clicks and glottal stops. And it's highly complex, as anthropologist Jay Powell found out as he grappled with it in the 1970s. Tribal elder Fred "Woody" Woodruff collaborated with Powell on a dictionary. This tome of 9,000 root words [only roughly 10 percent of the language] is now part of Quileute Tribal School curricula for K-12 youth: ***kikitalhil paqit***, or "geniuses at work."

RESERVATIONS

HOH In 1889, Washington State joined the Union, and 252 members of the Quileute Tribe found themselves assigned a 1-mile-square reservation on the mouth of the Quillayute. Four years later, 72 members of the **HOH BAND OF THE QUILEUTE** were recognized as a separate tribe and "provided" a 443-acre parcel one watershed south. Today, the Hoh are a sovereign nation of roughly 150 enrolled members. They remain a fishing people, bonded to the salmon, smelt, shellfish and cedarwood that have traditionally sustained P'ip'isodat'sili, or "Upside-Down People," as the Hoh sometimes call themselves. But the Hoh also contend with logging—60 percent of the Hoh basin is controlled as private and state timber holdings—and the complexities of being encircled by a national park.

QUINAULT At 325 square miles, the land of the **QUINAULT INDIAN NATION** is the third-largest reservation in Washington State, stretching from the Queets River south to Mocrocks Beach and east around Lake Quinault. The Nation's history with the U.S. government is one of broken promises. But QIN today is a powerhouse: one of the largest employers in Grays Harbor County, and the winner of legal battles like 1980's *United States v. Helen Mitchell*, which held the U.S. accountable for breach of trust and set a powerful precedent for other tribes.

ACTIVITIES

SURF AND OCEAN FISHING The remote, untrammeled nature of the Olympic beaches makes them a coveted angling destination. [Few sights capture the Pacific Northwest state of mind better than fisherfolk, geared up in waders, casting into iron-colored surf.] **RIALTO BEACH** is noted for redtail surfperch, and the hike north to Hole-in-the-Wall. **RUBY BEACH** is a stalking ground for sea-run cutthroat. For offshore missions in search of lingcod, rockfish and halibut, consult with Alpha Anglers of La Push. Always review national park [nps.gov/olym], Washington State [dfw.wa.gov] and tribal regulations—guidelines on specific species can change, year to year, season to season.

RIVER FISHING In this land of free-running rivers, the **HOH** stands apart for its reputation as a winter steelhead fishery—one of the West Coast's best—as well as for salmon and trout. The **WINTER STEELHEAD SEASON** runs approximately February to April. The management of this fishery, a collaboration between the state and the Hoh tribal government, is extraordinarily complex, undertaken with population levels in mind. For expert insight, see **MIKE Z'S GUIDE SERVICE**, a veteran outfit out of Forks with a keen eye for intricacies of land and water.

SHELLFISH GATHERING There's subtle Pacific Northwest street cred to owning a clam shovel, to say nothing of a "clam gun" or other specialized product. [Look into the **MURFF'S CLAMINATOR**, handcrafted stainless steel shovels from an Astoria, Oregon-based outfit.] **RAZOR CLAMS** are a popular quarry, drawing hundreds of springtime diggers to beaches like **KALALOCH** and, south of the park zone, **COPALIS** and Twin Harbors. The State of Washington monitors toxic acid levels in shellfish and opens and closes specific beaches on fairly short notice, with digging times synced to low tides, so consultation of dfw.wa.gov is mandatory.

WHALES

PACIFIC GRAY WHALES *migrate in spring, autumn and winter. Thousands travel from Alaska to Baja and back again, their coastal feeding making them a relatively common sight. A series of designated lookouts known as the* **WHALE TRAIL** *traces the coast.*

THE RAINFOREST

Among Olympic's many landscapes, the lush collage of rainforest in its western and southern reaches might be definitive. Mysterious and deep, a powerful visual clash of neon green and dark, wet woods, these forests hold some of the world's quietest places. These are our nation's richest remaining temperate rainforests—a vital resource for the planet, and endlessly intriguing to explore.

HISTORY

Kestner Homestead

Hike to ghostly settler remnants in the Quinault Rainforest.

CAMP

Hoh Oxbow

Site for tents and vehicles, deep in the woods.

NATURE

Banana slug

Ariolimax columbianus: native slimer, threatened by invasives.

HIKING TRAILS

BOGACHIEL RAINFOREST TRAIL #825

Entry point for several short-but-rugged loops, or takeoff point for backcountry journeys to the High Divide, elsewhere. "Bogachiel" likely derives from "muddy"—apt in many seasons.

QUINAULT LOOP

A 4-mile crash course in rainforest nature and aesthetics, skirting Lake Quinault before venturing into the woods, reaching lacy Cascade Falls. Intersects with Quinault Rain Forest Nature Trail.

5-MILE ISLAND

A 10-miler, round trip, but considered an easy classic on the Hoh River Trail. Bridges, waterfalls, and a view of Bogachiel Peak from the namesake campground. The Happy Four Shelter is just a bit further along.

EXPLORATION

THE HOH RIVER TRAIL: ROUTE TO OLYMPUS

One of the most contrast-packed expeditions in the American outdoors begins from the Hoh Rainforest, just 600 feet above sea level, and ascends to the peak of **MOUNT OLYMPUS**, the park's namesake. [That name was coined by John Meares, a rapscallion of a 18th-century colonial explorer, who observed its far-off snow capped peak from aboard the Felice Adventurer, a British ship masquerading as Portuguese ... and named it for Greek mythology. Strange times.] A five-day expedition to Olympus might begin at the Hoh Rainforest Visitor Center, ascending through the giant trees and pillowy moss to the **LEWIS MEADOW CAMPSITE**, a riverside respite. Further climbs lead into an alpine world of meadows and glacier views, notably the **BLUE GLACIER**, final objective for many ambitious backpackers. The final push to the summit requires technical climbing skills and gear and a full, rigorous day. For guided expeditionary outings to the mountain, consult:

PACIFIC ALPINE GUIDES
pacificalpineguides.com

NORTHWEST ALPINE GUIDES
northwestalpineguides.com

THE MOUNTAINEERS
mountaineers.org

In 1889, *the Seatte* Press *put out a stirring call to explorers willing to venture into the Olympics. By the following spring, the "Press Expedition" had survived six months in the mountains, after beginning in an exceptionally snowy December. The book* Across the Olympic Mountains *by Robert L. Wood [published by The Mountaineers] tells the tale.*

THE QUEETS RIVER TRAIL

While the Hoh has become one of the Northwest's most popular attractions for travelers, the lesser-known Queets requires determination to explore. The 22-mile out-and-back on the Queets River Trail only begins after fording both **SAMS RIVER** and the Queets River. [Don't attempt to ford if the river's running too high—summer is the safest season.] Wayfinding takes patience and sharp eyes, with champion Sitka spruce as the reward. The Queets is known as an attractive **PACKRAFTING** option: hike in, float out.

EXPLORATION

THE HOH

The park's iconic rainforest immersion.

The **HOH RAINFOREST** is, in fact, on land—we checked. But to wander this **UNESCO** heritage site is to feel deeply [if not directly] connected to the sea. A huge chunk of the Pacific lifts up and then falls down here, in the form of an absurd amount of rain: about 12 feet per year, official accounts report, not counting mists and fogs. That water sculpts dramatic solid forms, nourishing dense ferns, wizard-beard mosses shrouding gigantic trees and entire ecosystems [and soil types!] that exist high above in the forest canopy, never touching the loamy ground below. The National Park visitor center at the end of Hoh River Road has become one of the most popular attractions in the Pacific Northwest—visitation roughly tripled between 2011 and 2021—so planning is advised. A spring shoulder season excursion coincides with calving season for the Roosevelt elk that play a key ecological role in this landscape; fall foliage can be surprisingly vivid. But in any season, with any number of people, civilization melts away pretty fast in the **HALL OF MOSSES**, a loop short in distance but deep in mystical vibe, and the mandatory intro course on the Hoh. The **SPRUCE TRAIL** goes just a bit deeper into the woods, but still runs only a mile and change. The **HOH RIVER TRAIL** is the most robust route, running outward and upward toward Olympian heights.

In recent years, the Hoh has become renowned as "the quietest place in the United States" for its lack of human-created noise. Sound ecologist Gordon Hempton's book One Square Inch of Silence *explores the deeper importance of this serenity, and efforts to preserve it.*

BOGACHIEL RAINFOREST

North of the Hoh, the Bogachiel River flows from the highlands through lowland rainforest terrain. Lush hiking to be had, on sections of the longer Pacific Northwest Trail.

QUEETS RAINFOREST

Drive up rugged roads to throwback Queets Ranger Station [unstaffed]. The 3-ish-mile Sam's River Loop Trail explores tunnels of moss and far-flung riverbank.

HISTORY

LAKE QUINAULT

THE LAKE The pristine 3,000-acre lake sits in the southwest corner of the park in glacier-carved Quinault valley. This area is steeped in history—inhabited by the Quinault Indian Nation for thousands of years and used seasonally for the gathering of materials and food [berries, meat, fish]. The first documented white settler came to the valley in 1888 by way of the Quinault River. Still integral to the **QUINAULT INDIAN NATION**, the lake is enveloped by a temperate rainforest—the Quinault Rainforest. Today, sight the largest living Western red cedars, sitka spruces, Douglas firs, yellow cedars and mountain and Western hemlocks on the 31-mile loop around the lake. Or venture beyond the rocky shoreline on a paddleboard, kayak, or captained boat tour [book through Lake Quinault Lodge]. With a fishing permit from the Quinault Indian Nation, catch steelhead and trout [summer months only]. Lakeside camping is available at Gatton Creek.

THE LODGE In 1924, a fire ravaged the "Log Hotel" near Lake Quinault. Spinning this into an opportunity, lodge patrons began plans to replace this local institution. Nearly two years later—June 9, 1926—construction began on the new resort hotel, led by prominent Seattle architect **ROBERT REAMER.** By then, Reamer was renowned for his work in a new architectural style—known as National Park Rustic or, sometimes, as "parkitecture"—which emerged through Reamer's famed Old Faithful Inn in Yellowstone. Federal documents describe Reamer's work in the Olympic Peninsula as a marriage of the exterior and interior: "*This shingled lodge embracing a lawn leading down to the shore of Lake Quinault differs from Reamer's Yellowstone work, suggesting an attempt to mediate between human needs and the natural landscape of the Olympic Peninsula.*" The two-story lodge encapsulates the spirit of romanticized outdoorsmanship, with hand-crafted construction, woodland materials and Colonial Revival traditions [symmetry, gabled ends, a cupola]. Design and decorative nods to Native American culture are often of dubious authenticity, evoking a version of Mayan aesthetics in some analyses. Interesting to note: the lodge was completed in just 53 days to beat the formidable rainy season, with crews working through nights by bonfire light. On August 18, 1926, a grand opening celebration included 500 guests.

ROAD TRIP

Five days amid the shimmering waters, dense green forests and welcoming communities of Olympic country.

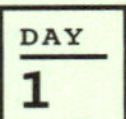

THE SOUND ODYSSEY

Trek up a corridor of water and woods to enter the Olympic realm and shellfish nirvana. Come as you are.

The **HOOD CANAL**, a glacier-scooped fjord slashed down Puget Sound's west side, works like a funnel. This mesmerizing waterway channels travelers and cultural energy through a narrow passage of small towns, fertile places and wildlands—and lays out an itinerary to briny finds and intriguing byways. Bring hiking boots and cooler for oysters.

10 A.M. Since 1890, family-owned **TAYLOR SHELLFISH** has defined the bounty of Northwest waters. Its small Shellfish Market in Sheldon is stocked deep with fresh oysters—Pacifics, Olympias and Kumamotos—to shuck as you will.

11 A.M. Hoodsport's **FJORD OYSTER BANK** satisfies immediate brine fever. Get three or a half-dozen on the half-shell, then browse this de facto cultural center's tiny bookstore.

LUNCH Among Northwest oysterfolk, all talk leads inevitably to **HAMA HAMA**. A bony mountain of shells marks the turn to the century-old outfit's Oyster Saloon. Check for serving hours for raw oysters and beer; shop the cold case, big tinned selection and live-crab tank.

1 P.M. Adventurers could take many worthy turns off the main route. Try **DUCKABUSH ROAD**, which quickly transforms from asphalt to a gravel wilderness portal. The **MURHUT FALLS TRAIL**, short but vigorous, ends at a mystical gusher in woods of deepest green.

3 P.M. After a call on Quilcene—a micro-cultural hub thanks to arts collective **GRAY COAST GUILDHALL**—detour on Center Road. **CHIMACUM** is quietly garnering a farm-to-fork reputation. Loop down Egg and I Road; stop in or call at Egg and I Pork for hazelnut-finished heritage meat. For free manure and compost offers, just keep your eyes open.

4:30 P.M. Just a glimpse of **FINNRIVER CIDER FARM** brings an easy sigh of relief after a day on road and trail. Gravel lot. Sprawling fields. Barnlike tasting room with ciders on tap. Order a pint in a mason jar, grab a picnic table and check the busy live-music schedule.

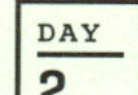

PORT TOWNSEND, THREE WAYS

A Victorian port town oozes history and charm. Walk it, then walk it some more.

DOWNTOWN

Staked out at the Sound's gateway during the Civil War, Port Townsend loomed large in settler dreams. Magnates and capitalists flocked, as did seafarers, saloon-keepers—you know the type—to create one of the West's most interesting wanders. Start at the sparkling **MARITIME CENTER**, a hangar of racing sculls and chandler's workshops marked by a Jamestown S'Kallam totem pole. Coffee at **VELOCITY** connects the dots of community—peruse posters for seamanship classes and rowing clubs, eavesdrop on cycling plans and art critiques. Weave between docks and piers and Water Avenue, soaking up salty ambience. Then, two bookstores will hold you for a bit. Indie gem **IMPRINT** has been in action since the '70s, with a strong showing of regional writers, small presses and Indigenous voices. Right across the street, **WILLIAM JAMES BOOKSELLER**, one of the great used bookstores: a cavernous trove, fathoms deep on every subject under the sun.

UPTOWN

An elegant vintage fountain on Washington Street marks the staircase climb to Uptown, originally Port Townsend's polite side. Today the mix feels charmingly vibrant: Finistere sets its fine-dining tables right across from treasured dive bar **UPTOWN PUB**, at the heart of Lawrence Street's shops and art stops. Above all, Uptown is a house-gawker's dream, with one imposing Victorian jewel after another. [The **STARRETT HOUSE**, built in 1889 and now a B & B, is a useful landmark.] Uptown tumbles down to the water at **CHETZEMOKA PARK**, a rambling domain of lapping waves, songbirds and deer.

FORT WORDEN

Port Townsend's strategic location once meant artillery up above town. Now, this old military base is a first-class place to ride a bike or hike an endless warren of trails to its spooky abandoned gun emplacements and bunkers. A collection of creative non-profits operates in the whitewashed Army buildings, including the Port Townsend School of Woodworking. Travelers can rent out old quarters for a key vantage of city and Sound.

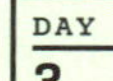

NORTHERN HIKES

The road from gateway town Port Angeles climbs into the National Park, reaching misty trailheads.

MARYMERE FALLS Like a 1970s soul classic, this jaunt out of the Lake Crescent area is smooth but heavy too. An easy-rolling trail, paved for much of the way, gently probes dense woods, connecting a workaday parking lot to the wilderness boundary. Things get more profound as wood-railed dirt stairs wind up to a view of the falls, coursing down over a stone cliff face livened up by neon moss.

STORM KING Branching off the Marymere Trail, here's something completely different: a 4-mile haymaker, round trip, involving notable scrambles over rocks and roots and lots of vigorous ascent [it climbs 1,700 feet]. The rewards: twisting madrona trees, gigantic cedars and views of Lake Crescent, opal-blue, below.

AURORA RIDGE This moss-lined magic carpet ventures through aspen stands, across numberless tiny creeks, the Sol Duc River rushing in the ravine below. Do a couple miles out and back, or keep going for longer adventures to Eagle Lake and Lake Crescent.

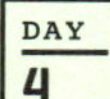

SURF THE WILD COAST

Venture to some of the West Coast's most far-flung places to catch a wave.

You wouldn't necessarily call the Olympic Peninsula a surf "scene." Combine the coast's long stretch of protected wilderness and the Northwest's reputation for fierce weather, and these become waves you have to earn. The obvious place to start is **LA PUSH**, the Quileute Reservation town at the literal end of the road from Forks. **FIRST BEACH**, the arc of coastline boarding the tiny hamlet to the west, offers the best-known beach break and the most reliable conditions. Rialto Beach also gets a nod if the stars [waves—you get the metaphor] align—rare. More intrepid souls can equip for **SHI SHI BEACH**, a hike-in only option. For rentals, lessons, retreats and an off-grid lodging option not far afield, check in with **LA PUSH SURF ADVENTURES**.

DAY 5

THE HOH RAIN FOREST

Water, wood and moss define Olympic's verdant heart.

Every big national park has its signature experience, whether that's Old Faithful's blast in Yellowstone, early light on Yosemite's Half Dome. In a park with Olympic's diverse landscapes, it could be hard to pick just one. Except the **HOH RAIN FOREST** exists: this park's visual crescendo.

The undulating **HOH VALLEY ROAD**, along the braided Hoh River, makes a worthy journey in itself. For a surreal commemoration of history, pause at the **NIKOLAI MEMORIAL**, a kiosk of plaques telling of a Russian colonial ship run aground in 1808, and its crew's desperate times on the peninsula. [Along with the remarkable tale, this is for sure the only place in the world you'll see the flags of Russia, Washington State and the Quileute and Hoh tribes fly next to each other.]

The park's **HOH VALLEY VISITOR CENTER** anchors one of the Northwest's most popular travel destinations. Popular for good reason: In an average year, 140 inches of rain fall here, lifeblood of continental America's finest surviving temperate rainforest. Ecologists have lately identified this dense, teeming collection of ancient trees as a key to mitigating climate change. From soil fungi to mosses and lichens in staggering variety to the Roosevelt elk browsing its understory, the forest is an ark of complex life. The first impression, however, is simple enough: the place looks amazing.

Take the short and easy **HALL OF MOSSES TRAIL**, where trees tower and twist under veils of psychedelic green. Many of the octopus-limbed maples here suggest fairy-tale creatures, maybe ominous ones. But all this pillowy moss and the lulling pulse of flowing water make this a place of softness, a wilderness that feels as gentle as it is humbling. [Just the root structures of some of the fallen nurse logs, which sprout whole glades of younger trees, stand double or triple an average human's height.]

Hikes get a little longer, in the form of the **SPRUCE NATURE TRAIL** [just over a mile], or much longer, in the form of the **HOH RIVER TRAIL**. The latter stretches 18 miles up to the glaciers of Mount Olympus—a different biome, in other words. If you're up for that, it's a path that will give you Olympic in full.

BASE CAMPS

Much of the park itself is remote wilderness, untracked by roads. But paradoxically, the Olympic Peninsula and the Northwest at its borders are human wonderlands, too: creative small-town charm, ancesteral communities and even a couple shiny metropoles.

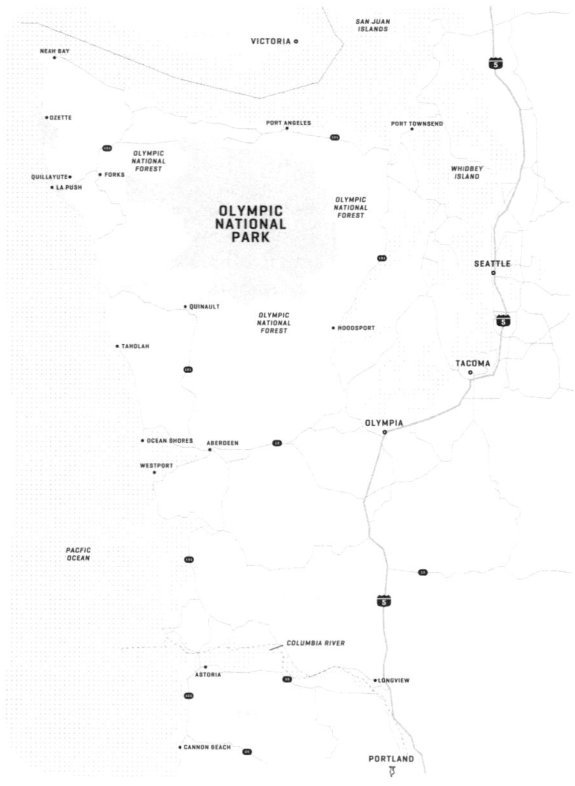

SEATTLE

Look west—from Discovery Park, say, with its 500 acres of urban nature—and the Olympic Mountains glitter across Puget Sound. Turn inland to admire the most impressive U.S. skyline north of San Francisco. Seattle may be a hyper-modern tech hub, but deep down it remains a rugged outpost of seafaring, mountain climbing and gold-rush history. **PIKE PLACE MARKET** is an orientation point, historic open-air counters leading to endless-feeling corridors and backstreets. **THE CENTER FOR WOODEN BOATS**' rentals can get you out on Sound waters; the roadie fleet at cycling mecca **METIER** unlocks the city's hills. In the beachy Alki neighborhood, **DRIFTWOOD** roams from Sound shellfish to Makah black cod to bounty from island and valley farms—menus that weave together all the Seattle threads.

MICROBREWERY	POPULATION: 749,256
Holy Mountain	COFFEE: Mr. West, Caffe Vita at KEXP
Near-mystical small-batch pints	BEST DAY OF THE YEAR: Bumbershoot Music Fest, September

PORTLAND

Three hours' drive northward takes a traveler from Portland to Olympic National Park. But head other directions, and the same road time puts you in Bend's sagey high desert. Or oceanfront sand dunes near Florence. Or the pines of Gifford Pinchot National Forest. The point is: Portland is a base for many expeditions. **MOUNTAIN SHOP** is a venerable outfitter on the East Side; **NEXT ADVENTURE** is famed for its packed bargain basement of gear. Without leaving city limits, ramblers can wander **FOREST PARK**'s 80 miles of densely wooded trails, then emerge practically straight onto the Providence Park terraces for a **PORTLAND TIMBERS** soccer match, or front-door at **BREAKSIDE BREWERY**. The mod-hostel **KEX** was built with light travelers in mind.

FESTIVE NIGHT	POPULATION: 635,067
Gado Gado	COFFEE: Carnelian, Guilder, Electrica
Crew up for the Indonesian "rice table" feast	BEST DAY OF THE YEAR: First ride of Pedalpalooza, June

PORT TOWNSEND

This Victorian seaport wears its history like a jaunty top hat, championing arts, culture, food and drink. But even in its refined heart, this town has a wild side. [Start with the hordes of deer browsing yards and parks.] The 135-mile **OLYMPIC DISCOVERY TRAIL**, a coveted cycling route, begins here and goes all the way to La Push. The sea kayaks of **OLYMPIC KAYAK TOURS** depart from Fort Flagler, just north, seeking bioluminescent sea life; excursions with **SAIL PORT TOWNSEND** or the Northwest Maritime Center's catamaran day trips put you in the salt air. Almost 12 miles of hiking trails thread atmospheric **FORT WORDEN**, perched above town. A fish-and-chips basket might sound perfect after all this; head for **DOC'S MARINA GRILL**.

ARTS ORG	
Northwind *Classes and exhibits with flair*	POPULATION: 10,306 COFFEE: Velocity, Better Living Through Coffeee BEST DAY OF THE YEAR: Wooden Boat Festival, September

PORT ANGELES

The park's northern gateway is the ungentrified Northwest. Pickups and logging trucks rumble the main drag; the **BLACK BALL FERRY** chugs to and from Victoria, British Columbia. The sparkling new **FIELD HALL** performance venue brings impressive shine, but for our money **COOG'S BUDGET RECORDS** is the true cultural find, a basement lair of physical media [360-457-9211]. Fortify for the park at **NEXT DOOR GASTROPUB** or the self-explanatory **BARBECUE**, at least until the Memphis-style meat runs out. Gear questions find solutions at **BROWN'S OUTDOOR** and Waters West Fly Fishing Outfitters. Stock up on gorp, trail bars and sandwiches at crunchy grocery **COUNTRY AIRE**. **PORT BOOK AND NEWS** gathers a rich batch of science and naturalist titles.

SURF & TURF	
Kokopelli Grill *The long-running local favorite*	POPULATION: 20,060 COFFEE: Easy Street BEST DAY OF THE YEAR: Maritime Festival, June

LA PUSH

The Quileute Nation's headquarters is simultaneously a natural wonder, remote fishing village, ancient cultural center and modern sovereign land. **FIRST BEACH**, curving between dramatic haystack rocks, defines the town. Surfers and fisherfolk people its hypnotic waves. Tribe-owned **QUILEUTE OCEANSIDE RESORT** makes a homey refuge, with spotless rooms and generous kitchen setups. Its office sells select Northwest Coast art mementos and books, and provides guidance on visiting this Indigenous community—the etiquette of photography, campfires and the like. Cozy **RIVER'S EDGE RESTAURANT** is the one and only dining game, but for smoked salmon, fresh-catch and fishing charters, ask around.

CHINESE	
Golden Gate *A throwback Szechuan find in nearby Forks*	POPULATION: 416 COFFEE: Native Grounds Espresso BEST DAY OF THE YEAR: Quileute Days, July

WESTPORT

To all appearances, Westport is sleepy, unfancy, somewhat remotely tucked the edge of vast Grays Harbor. Untouched by trendiness, unfazed by hipness. And yet three surf breaks and year-round waves have created a pathway between this fishing town and the world. The burgeoning scene is most evident at **LOGE**, a made-over motel with a mod-surf-camp vibe, and the gear-rental shop **STEEPWATER**. After the waves, repair to Blackbeard's Brewing for refreshment, or seek old-school seafood-shack stylings at **BENNETT'S**. The most singular dining experience in these parts lies down the road at **THE WANDERING GOOSE** [a.k.a. the Tokeland Hotel]. Seattle-minted chef Heather Earnhardt puts local oysters and rockfish into a homespun Southern vernacular.

HISTORY SPOT	
Westport Maritime Museum *Displays the lighthouse lens from Destruction Island*	POPULATION: 2,254 COFFEE: Green Monster BEST DAY OF THE YEAR: Annual driftwood show, August

OLYMPIA

Washington State's capital is a low-key place. But secretly, this is a cultural powerhouse with exceptional impact-per-capita. Indie music is at the core of this alternative story: record labels **KILLROCKSTARS** and **K RECORDS**; the Riot Grrl movement and Nirvana's origins. Hit **LE VOYEUR** for live shows; dig in the stacks at **RAINY DAY RECORD CO.** and **LANTERN RECORDS**. Evergreen State College's **KAOS** is a vintage college radio station, with a locals-driven program list that matches the call letters. The commitment to creativity spans eras, too **BROWSER'S BOOKSTORE** dates to the 1930s, while **LAST WORD BOOKS** reflects the town's 21st Century bohemian leanings. Open the shell on another dimension of Northwest culture at **CHELSEA FARMS OYSTER HOUSE**.

EXCURSIONS	
Olympia Sailing Company *Day-sail the Sound on a vintage schooner.*	POPULATION: 55,919 COFFEE: Ember Goods BEST DAY OF THE YEAR: Olympia Harbor Days, September

HOODSPORT

At first glance, this is the proverbial wide spot in the road, a hamlet squeezed between the looming Olympic wilderness and the spectacular fjord Hood Canal. There's more here than meets the eye, though, starting beneath the waves at **SUND ROCK MARINE PRESERVE**, a magnet for scuba enthusiasts seeking entry to the domain of the mighty wolf eel [and myriad other creatures]. Indeed, Hoodsport is all about the meeting of land and sea—vividly so at **SUNRISE RESORT**, a chill abode slung along the waterfront and base for boating, diving, crabbing and oystering. The **FJORD OYSTER BANK** and **POTLATCH BREWING** are the yin and yang of brine and hops here. Head inland and upward to bask in the glow of Lake Cushman, a summer weekenders' staple.

SPIRITS	
Hardware Distillery *Aquavit enhances the Scandinavian vibe.*	POPULATION: 139 COFFEE: Hoodsport Coffee Co. BEST DAY OF THE YEAR: Fjordin Crossin paddling challenge, June

NEAH BAY

The far, far corner of the contiguous United States: untouched by roads until the 1930s. Today's Neah Bay has a handful of streets, a marina, and, on clear days, views of Vancouver Island. Once one of the Makah Tribe's five primary villages, it's now part of the reservation; alcohol is not sold or legal here, and a Makah recreation permit is required at trails and beaches. At the **MAKAH CULTURAL & RESEARCH CENTER**, study artifacts—whale-hunting tools, sealing spears, cedar baskets, mussel-shell knives. Tear into fry bread at **PAT'S PLACE** or fish and chips at **CALVIN'S CRAB HOUSE** from Adirondack chairs overlooking the Strait of Juan de Fuca. Three miles southwest, **HOBUCK BEACH RESORT** offers Pacific-facing cabins and campsites.

HALIBUT HOOKUP	
Windsong Charters	POPULATION: 1,079
Fishing trips, whale watching, sunset tours	COFFEE: Native Grounds Espresso
	BEST DAY OF THE YEAR: Makah Days Celebration, late August

ASTORIA

Due south of the wild Olympic coast, across the Columbia River's fearsome mouth ["Graveyard of the Pacific"], Astoria is a bastion of Northwest lore. Lewis & Clark ended up here; **GOONIES** made the town a Gen-X pop culture staple. The atmospheric town remains the real deal even as it gets a bit glossier. Downtown shelters both modern boho shopping [**SHORT WAVE**] and nods to sea-salty history [**FLAVEL HOUSE MUSEUM**, once a captain's abode]. For pure spirit, however, it's hard to beat **DEAD MAN'S ISLE**, a cozy bolthole that translates tiki-bar tropicalia for these stormier, mistier climes. Order a Nielson's Blood or Blackbeard's Ghost. Just across the river, Japanese gear brand Snow Peak recently opened **LONG BEACH CAMPFIELD**, a luxe-rustic retreat.

FROZEN TREAT	
Custard King	POPULATION: 10,343
Roadside soft-serve: a local icon	COFFEE: Coffee Girl
	BEST DAY OF THE YEAR: Astoria Regatta, August

INCLUDING

INTERVIEWS

Twelve conversations with locals of note about the arts, rain, Indigenous culture, silence, oysters, backcountry adventure and more.

NIKKI MCCLURE

ARTIST

I DRAW A SKETCH, and then I transfer that sketch to black paper. Then, I cut out shapes with an X-Acto knife.

I HAVE TO distill the image to its essence. The limit is a challenge, and I like that.

I DIDN'T HAVE an art background at all. I studied natural history. So, my knowledge is in the difference between a hazelnut twig and a vine maple twig in winter, or a Brewer's blackbird and the brown-headed cowbird.

WHEN IT CAME time for college, I only applied to Evergreen.

I HAD HEARD that there were no grades. And that you didn't have to declare a major. And that you got to call your professors by their first name.

I'D BEEN GOING to punk shows in Seattle—the shaking, nervous girl from the suburbs in these intense spaces. I knew the shows in Olympia were better. I don't know how I knew that. I just did.

BEAT HAPPENING'S first album has a picture on the back cover: Bret and Heather and Calvin on these railroad tracks in downtown Olympia. It was like a beacon: a siren call to me to come to that railroad trestle.

YOU WERE ALWAYS making something. It was always on. Almost like we would write songs rather than talk, or make a picture rather than call someone.

ALSO, WE REALLY only got one TV channel. When *The Simpsons* came on, everyone would watch *The Simpsons*. Otherwise, we had to entertain ourselves.

ABOUT 10 YEARS ago, I was at an age where people were saying, "How are your eyes? How are your eyes?"

THE DOCTOR SAYS, "Your eyes are incredible." Like, I could see every little braid of detail in a cedar tree, far away.

EVERY NEEDLE OF a fir tree, every rain drop on it.

TOMMY FARRIS

HIKING GUIDE

YOU CAN EXPLORE a temperate rainforest in the morning and go tidepooling on the Wilderness Coast in the afternoon.

IN WINTER, you could go snowshoeing in the morning and surfing in the afternoon.

YOU SEE PEOPLE truly disconnect, get lost in their own minds.

THERE'S A UNIQUE window to getting into the backcountry mountains. Snowmelt typically makes it really accessible from mid-July to mid-September. It can spill into October.

IN EARLY OCTOBER, you see the colors transition from the vibrant green and wildflowers of summer into reds and golds.

THE ONLY WAY to connect these places is to see them on foot. You have to go up into the highlands, then back down into the lowland valleys.

I'M TRYING TO put together the perfect puzzle, and figure out how to knock out every mile of backcountry trail in the park. How to weave them all together.

YOU HAVE TO be prepared for any change of weather. Snow can stick around into July—are you ready to encounter snow?

ON THE COAST, the tide schedule is the single most important piece of information.

BETWEEN OIL CITY and Third Beach, you have to get past Diamond Rock. That requires a two-foot tide or lower.

SOME PARTS OF the year, there might not be a tide during daylight hours that goes below two feet—for a week at a time.

SEEING A BULL elk on the Hall of Mosses trail. Seeing a black bear cross the trail on the Seven Lakes Basin Loop.

SEEING BLUE GLACIER up close for the first time.

LONI GRINNELL-GRENINGER

TRIBAL VICE CHAIRWOMAN

AS SOVEREIGN NATIONS, we have the ability to govern ourselves, to have jurisdiction over our people and our ancestral lands.

WE LOOK AT Creation through a familial lens. We view Creation as brothers, sisters, aunties uncles, grandparents.

STORIES SHOW THAT we viewed creatures through the lens of being actual people—that they could be the village of the Orca People, the village of the Salmon People, the Bear People, the Wolf People.

THEY COULD BE a salmon, and then they could come on land and be human, and they could go back to being a salmon again.

THE JAMESTOWN S'Klallam Tribe governs our service and enterprises toward serving people and taking care of the land.

WITH THE FOREST Service and the National Park, the tribe doesn't own the deed anymore.

FOR THE SAKE of having a relationship with our land, we will keep coming to the table.

WHAT DOES IT mean to help tourists, guests of the forest? Help them take care of the land?

I WAS APPOINTED when I was 29. It was January 2020. There was a steep learning curve.

I LOVE BEING with my people. I also like being at the table with all these other governments.

I ALSO LOVE watching the three sister tribes—Lower Elwha Klallam, the Port Gamble S'Klallam, ourselves—work together more and more.

MY GRANDFATHER from seven generations ago was one of the local chiefs . His name is čičməhán, and he signed the Point No Point Treaty in 1855.

MY GRANDMA WAS on tribal council, my dad was on tribal council. And now I'm on tribal council.

GORDON HEMPTON

SOUND ECOLOGIST

LET ME MEET myself as an ancient body. What are my instincts telling me about Olympic National Park? Is it safe? Is it prosperous?

BASED ON THE sounds, if I were suddenly stranded here, could I live here for months?

EVERY PLACE ON Planet Earth sounds different. Sound is produced by events. Sound carries information. So acoustic ecology answers the questions: Who is listening? Why are they listening?

MOSTLY I LISTEN to unintentional sounds. The background sounds. You can listen to any place, whether it's a city or a wilderness—any place in the world—and learn lots of things.

I'VE REFERRED TO Olympic National Park as "the listeners' Yosemite." It's sonically the most diverse American national park with wilderness areas.

THERE'S THE ALPINE region, with the creaking and cracking of glaciers. The endemic marmot makes a sound that is one of the most information-dense communications in the world.

THEN WE HAVE the most extensive coniferous forest in all of the United States. Virgin forest.

I COULD GO on and on about when you hear elk bugle. A lovely experience—but very different if you're close to the elk. I don't recommend that.

IF YOU'RE CLOSE to an elk when it bugles, your body will tell you whether or not it's a good idea to be there at that moment.

SOUND TELLS US a wave crashed on the beach. Sound tells us whether the beach was sand, pebble or rock. Is it a high-energy beach, exposed to the large Pacific swells? Or a low-energy beach?

NOT ONLY DOES it take the entire Pacific Northwest to produce a place like this, it takes the whole planet.

GARY MORISHIMA

ADVISOR, QUINAULT INDIAN NATION

I'VE BEEN ASSOCIATED with the Quinault Nation since the late 1960s. I started out working to set up the Natural Resources Department.

THAT WAS A time of great change and controversy. Demonstrations and violence happened: the Alcatraz occupation, the takeover of the Bureau of Indian Affairs in the early '70s. There was the controversy at Pine Ridge in 1975, and the Boldt case, which affirmed treaty fishing rights in Western Washington.

THERE WAS A great movement within Indian Country to change the policy of the United States. The president of the Quinault Indian Nation was at the forefront of that.

THE INFLUENCE OF Quinault goes beyond the region, to the national and international level.

QUINAULT LEADERSHIP, going back into the '60s, recognized that it needed to become recognized as a government, on equal footing with the states and the federal government.

IT'S A DIFFERENT kind of a worldview. It's an understanding that for too long tribal peoples have been subject to suppression, domination and displacement.

TRIBES LIVED AND interacted with their environment. They lived in villages along the rivers, fishing, hunting and gathering.

THAT WORLD WAS governed by traditions, customs, practices and traditional knowledge accumulated over millennia. They had their own systems of tribal justice to maintain social order.

THAT CHANGED UPON contact with Europeans.

TODAY, TRIBES ARE active leaders in terms of climate change, for example. How do we continue to try to protect and care for the environment? To recognize an obligation and a relationship that has to be sustained over generations?

LYNN MCMURDIE

PRECIPITATION SCIENTIST

STORMS HAVE nuances, variability. Storms are just like people—they change.

THEY COMPLETELY reinvent themselves on the east side of the Rockies, and turn into some other completely different behemoth over Minnesota. Who knows what happens next?

I'M INTO ANYTHING to do with precipitation, liquid or frozen.

WASHINGTON IS A land of contrasts. It has a temperate rainforest, rainy systems that happen for nine months of the year. Ocean, dry grasslands, dense fog.

THE STORMS HERE, they change so much. They come here on the West Coast, and then they hobble over to the eastern part of our state.

MY COLLEAGUE Bob Houze was involved with NASA, measuring precipitation from space. He approached me. He was doing a field campaign on the Olympic Peninsula.

WE WANTED TO understand how storm systems change when they're over the ocean and approach land.

WHY DOES IT rain a lot more on the windward slopes, versus the top of the mountains, versus on the lee side?

THERE'S QUITE A strong change across the crest of the high terrain of the Olympics.

WHEN WE TALK about all the heavy rains that happen there, it's on the western side.

WHEN YOU GO to the northeast corner of the peninsula—like Sequim and Port Angeles—that doesn't get very much rain at all. It's blocked by the high terrain.

THEY GET 18 inches of rain a year. The coast gets over 100 inches.

WOULD YOU LIKE to be in my world? Well, you just look up. Every time I step outside, I'm looking up.

JENNY WADDELL

ECOLOGIST

THIS COASTLINE IS littered with rocks and hazards. For mariners and navigators, it's just a landmine of rocks. It'll sink your ship real quick.

BIG STORMS ROLL in with little warning. We've got high currents, lots of rocks, lots of giant waves. It is not a place for beginners.

THE OLYMPIC COAST National Marine Sanctuary covers almost half the coast of Washington: Nearly 3,200 square miles, which is a whole lot of ocean.

WE HAVE A very small team, and I am in charge of coordinating natural, environmental research, and a bit of social science as well—maritime heritage, things like that.

HOW MUCH dissolved oxygen is in the water? How warm are the temperatures? Salinity, temperature, oxygen, ocean acidification.

PROBABLY 95 PERCENT of the population of Washington sea otters is found within the sanctuary. They do things here that they don't seem to do in other places, I think because there aren't great white sharks here.

THEY FORM GIANT rafts of animals that all float together. Some of these rafts are hundreds and hundreds of animals. One of them that we counted was 682 otters all just floating together like three miles offshore.

WE DO A lot of work sending robots to the very depths of the ocean.

DEEP SEA CANYONS bisect the continental shelf. Within those canyons are amazing, fantastical aggregations of deep sea corals and sponges.

THE ROBOTS GET all kinds of cool video of deep sea corals and sponges and animals living at 5,000 feet in the depths of Quinault Canyon.

HUGE BUBBLEGUM CORALS. Giant sponges of various types

and shapes, many of which are new to science.

IN 2018, I was contacted by NASA's cosmic dust curator. A massive meteorite had exploded and fallen into the sanctuary.

WE HAD MAGNETIC wands. We had scoopers. We had a slurp machine. We had a mini dredge.

WE HAD AN industrial magnet that we had shipped over from Europe.

NO ONE HAD ever recovered a meteorite from the ocean floor.

PRISCIDIA MCCARTY

ARTIST

IF I COULD watch my whole life as a movie, childhood would be the part I would watch the most.

I GOT TO live on my ancestral land. I would fall asleep to the sounds of the ocean.

I WAS JUST hanging out in the woods with the dogs.

WE HAD CULTURE class every single day instead of history class. We just learned about Makah.

MY DAD WOULD be in the shop carving. If it was raining, I'd go sit in there with him.

HE WOULD HAVE me use the bandsaw and cut out blocks, and do a lot of shaping. Basically stuff that I couldn't mess up.

A LOT OF sanding. A lot of finishing work and beginning work.

HE'D GIVE ME some sandpaper and be like, "All right, fix the edges, fix the creases, because I'm old and blind."

LATELY I'VE BEEN doing a lot of beading. The Jamestown S'klallam Tribe requested a bunch of necklaces.

MY PARENTS STARTED me and my older sister off with plastic beads.

EVERY SUMMER WE would say, "All right, we got to get this ready for Makah Days."

MY DAD WAS LIKE, "Yes, it's a really good creative outlet." And my mom would say, "Yeah, a creative outlet that makes money."

I DON'T REALLY do a whole lot of traditional stuff. It has a bunch of Makah elements in it. I always want to try new things.

I STRUGGLE TO get my art in museums.

THEY SAY PEOPLE won't buy because it isn't authentic.

I SAY, "WELL, I'm an authentic Makah. That's what it is."

LOWELL SKOOG

MOUNTAINEERING HISTORIAN

THE OLYMPICS WERE this forgotten backwater. The mysterious range of the Northwest.

LEWIS AND CLARK had seen Mount Hood and Mount Saint Helens. The Cascades are named for the Columbia River, which they also navigated. But the Olympics were only sighted by ship's captains offshore.

REAL EXPLORATION didn't start until the 1880s.

THERE WERE NO railroads going through, no significant mining interests.

THE OLYMPICS WERE never really developed for skiing like the Cascades. But interestingly, there was a community that wanted to ski.

DEER PARK WAS a little ski area in the 1930s and '40s. I talked to people who were around then, just before or just after the war, and they would describe how hair-raising it was to go up the road. People would break their chains.

IN 1957 AND '58, there was the International Geophysical Year. A team spent the whole year on Mount Olympus—they built a cabin up on the snow dome.

THEY GOT PERMISSION to fly in and out: the first glacier landing by a plane in Washington State.

PEOPLE DO GET in there to climb or ski, but you have to hike.

MOUNT OLYMPUS IS the classic example—it's almost a 20-mile hike just to get to Blue Glacier.

YOU'RE WALKING among these gigantic trees and mossy forests. Very gradually, you climb up the alpine zone.

BLUE GLACIER SPILLS off of this shoulder of Mount Olympus, and then comes down this really flat tongue that is unique.

THE BIG VOLCANOES don't have a glacier like that.

SO FLAT THAT it looks like an ice field.

SARA MACIAS

INNKEEPER

MIKE'S BEACH RESORT was a gastro tourism place before anybody was using that word.

IN THE 1950s, people would come to stay and get oysters on the beach. Word of mouth.

WHEN MIKE'S STARTED, it was just three small wooden cabins. No electricity. No running water.

MY GRANDFATHER WAS an avid scuba diver.

RIGHT OUT FRONT, on Hood Canal, there is a protected marine park. People come to see the giant Pacific octopus.

HE BEGAN TO build cabins. They named the place after their first and only son, Mike—my dad.

FOLKS WOULD trailer up here, enjoy the water, go swimming, have campfires. And scuba, of course.

"GOOD, OLD-FASHIONED family fun on the Highway 101." That was their little tagline.

THE CORE OF what Mike's Beach Resort is all about hasn't changed. It's been enhanced.

NOW WE DO yoga retreats, writing retreats, weddings, events.

YOU KNOW WHAT it is? An answer to a call. I need to reconnect with myself. Reconnect with the natural world.

IT'S MY MOM and my dad and my brother and my husband. We have two children, as well as my sister-in-law and my nephew.

SEVEN AND A HALF years ago, we had all these customers telling us we have the best oysters—what about selling in restaurants?

WE CREATED Olympic Oyster Company. We started cold-calling at restaurants, and got kicked out of most of them. We'd be dripping oyster water all over the floor.

IT TOOK JUST one chef to say, "Okay, let's crack one of these puppies open."

MICHAEL TAPPEL

TRAIL RUNNER

"FASTEST KNOWN TIME" as a concept has been around for a while, but it really caught on during the pandemic.

MOST PEOPLE DO them unsupported. Carrying their own gear. Drinking from streams.

YOU HAVE TO tap into different sources of energy and motivation. You thought you hit bottom, but you have to keep going.

I LOVE GETTING to places that a day-hiker wouldn't reach.

THE GRAND LOOP is a 43-ish-mile loop on the north end of Olympic National Park. It has 13,000 feet of vertical gain—quite a lot for that distance.

THE FIRST HALF, you're going along beautiful ridges with panoramic vistas of the Olympics.

THE SECOND HALF, you drop down into lower valleys, running along streams, running through that classic Olympic lush green rainforest.

I WENT INTO it thinking, "For the first 20 miles, I'm not even going to look at my watch."

YOU'RE HIGH ON these ridges. Amazing mountain views, great wildflowers.

I HIT THE first big turn. I looked at my watch. I was 15 or 20 minutes under the time. Okay, now we're racing.

THERE WERE MOMENTS when I felt really miserable. But my mantra is to never make any decisions on an uphill.

GET TO THE top, eat something, drink some water, start running down. Take stock.

I TAGGED THE sign at the trailhead, and then just sat down in this gravel parking lot.

BUT I HAD friends back at the camp. They all look at me and don't say anything.

AND THEN I SAID, "I got it." So there was a small celebration.

JANINE LEDFORD

HISTORIAN

I GREW UP in Neah Bay, and we would regularly visit Ozette.

THE EXCAVATION AT Ozette started in 1970. We'd see how they were excavating, and you got to learn about archaeology as a kid. And of course, we knew that Makah elders were involved and that young Makah people were always working alongside the field-school students.

WHEN YOU'RE YOUNG, you think this exists everywhere. As I matured, I realized, oh, not every tribe has an active archaeological site you get to visit regularly.

I LEARNED TO weave baskets when I was young. So by the time I was in fifth and sixth grade, I was able to help with making some and harpoon sheets—some of the cedar bark replicas that are on display in our museum.

IN THE '70s, we had wonderful Makah elders working in the school, and we could sit with them and weave baskets and learn language.

ONE OF THE women that I learned to weave baskets from was born the same year as my great-grandma.

AFTER COLLEGE, I came back and started working for the museum right away.

WHEN I WAS YOUNG, we were all sort of exposed to Makah words and phrases. Most kids around here grow up with a certain Makah vocabulary. To jump to the present, we have a language program within the Makah Cultural and Research Center.

YOU'RE LEARNING so much more as you're learning language. You're learning about culture and history, values and identity, resources and foods.

SCHOOL'S NOT THE only place to learn language. But schools were used as agents of language destruction for so many decades. Now, they take some responsibility for language revitalization.

INCLUDING

STORIES

Essays and poems from writers with deep perspectives on the Olympic Peninsula.

YOU CAN EAT THE VIEW

Written by ROWAN JACOBSEN

THE MISGIVINGS USUALLY START sometime after you trade the interstate for U.S. 101, the road that loops the Olympic Peninsula like a lariat. Whatever city you launched from—Seattle, Tacoma, Portland—conditions were better, and somehow you thought that would translate to the Olympics, not so far away in real miles.

But now here you are, hugging 101 for dear life as it threatens to pitch you into the whitecapped teeth of Hood Canal at every turn, and you are remembering for the umpteenth time that things are different out here. The jagged white peaks ghosting out of the clouds. The moss-bright woods. The glacial creeks pouring meltwater into the canal, which is really a fjord, the name a mistranslation of the original "Hood's Channel" George Vancouver penned into his 1792 journal. It's as if you've slipped back in time to some primordial landscape when the world was young and still in the process of being made. And really all you were looking for was a plate of oysters and a beer.

Steady on. Stick with your instincts. The oysters are there. *Everywhere*, in fact. If it's low tide, you'll catch them out of the corner of your eye as you negotiate another hairpin turn. Hood Canal is one of the great places on the planet to harvest wild oysters. The cobbly delta of every creek seems to be coated in them. But, well, you forgot your boots, you never bought your shellfish license, and anyway, it's 37 frigging degrees and the low tide's at midnight. There are easier ways.

Not that it's going to be *that* easy. Your destination—the Hama Hama Saloon—is entirely outdoors, a few dozen picnic tables stashed between the shell piles and the water. It's a natural outgrowth of the Hama Hama oyster farm, a barnacle attached to the shucking house, a pipeline from the oyster beds to your mouth, and it falls high on the Northwest life list. Which means that on any given Sunday in summer, half of Seattle has had the exact same idea.

But you have outsmarted them all by coming ... now. No crowds! You bask in your cleverness as sleet beads off your windshield.

But beating the crowd is just part of your master plan. You've done your homework. You know that in high summer, oysters are skinny, having exhausted themselves to reproduce. In winter, however, they are plump and sweet, filled with the energy stores that are going to get them through the dark days when there isn't much algae to eat. You are here to taste perfection.

Your mouth starts to water as you come around the final curve and the handmade roadside signs begin. "Hama Hama Seafood 1/4 mile." "Oysters." "Clams." "Crab."

You pull into the gravel parking lot beside the shell mountain strewn with oyster gear and what looks like a WWII landing craft, and throw on yet another parka to defend against the icy ... *snain, perhaps*? ... spitting out of the sky.

Unbelievably, you are not alone. A half dozen cars fill the parking lot, their people gabbing boisterously at picnic tables set beneath plywood A-frames along the shore. Servers in Grundens forge through the squall to deliver piles of bivalves. Everyone looks like they just came off a mountaineering expedition. Everyone has oyster juice in their beards. You feel that you have penetrated to the heart of the Olympic Peninsula.

You step up to a kiosk and order raw Hamas on the halfshell and grilled Hamas with chipotle bourbon sauce and a smoked oyster salad. And then, because you're freezing, you add a steaming bowl of chowder and some purple savory clams in curry broth. Then you grab your can of Oyster Bro Pilsner and head for your table.

If it's low tide, the oyster beds stretch out beside you, the crews picking the beach and piling clams and oysters into metal totes with buoys attached. If it's high tide, Adam James will be out in the Hama Hama barge, lifting those totes onto the deck. With his exuberant mustache and gunslinger vibe, Adam could step seamlessly into any of the five generations of family photographs lining the shucking house walls, dating back to the 1890s, when Washington was barely a state and Adam's family first bought this land. Back then, they weren't thinking about oysters. They were working the miles of beautiful timber filling the Hamma Hamma River valley. Only in the 1950s did they turn their attention to the shells carpeting the river delta.

There are establishments that spring from nothingness to fill some perceived demographic longing. This would describe 90 percent of the restaurants that fill your Instagram feed or the review columns of major publications. And then there are those that just happen over time, an accretion of microresponses to changing conditions. Hama Hama is one of the latter. For 66 years, it has stayed glued to this spot, like an oyster itself, responding to whatever good things drift by.

For a long time, the oyster business was a volume game. Hama Hama shucked oysters into gallon buckets and sold them to distributors by the truckload. Then all the neighbors were stopping by the shucking house to buy a bag of oysters for their party, and the packers were getting sick of taking off their gloves to make the sale, so in the '70s Hama Hama built a little farm store. And of course the parade of cars just grew, so they added clams and smoked oysters and started selling their friends' salmon and Dungeness and Douglas-fir jelly. And then they built a bigger farm store.

Then in the 2000s, halfshell culture exploded in the U.S. and people went goofy for that Hama flavor of salt and stone and whatever green magic is pouring out of the Olympics. And suddenly, writers and restaurateurs were making the pilgrimage, and by the 2010s Xtratuf and Patagonia were shooting ads with the farm crew, and Outstanding in the Field was throwing dinners on the tidelands, and Hama Hama had become a state of mind, a windswept lifestyle, and the trucker hats just wouldn't stay on the shelves.

And of course everybody wanted to eat their oysters outside the store, looking over the canal, so just for fun, the gang set up a grill and filled it with oysters on weekends, and let's just say that was not unpopular, so they gave in to the inevitable and added the "saloon"—really just some picnic tables, a rope, and a liquor license—and, well, you see how these things happen. The plywood A-frames were simply a stopgap, but now everyone finds them adorable, a little pointy forest to match the one rising on the other side of 101, so they might just stay a while.

As might you. You've just drained your Oyster Bro and noticed that the mustachioed mountain man on the can is actually Adam James—an homage from Shelton's High Steel Brewing Company—when your raw oysters show up. Thanks, yes, you'll take another beer.

You drip Douglas-fir mignonette onto your Hama Hamas and

slide one into your mouth, keeping one eye peeled for orcas in the canal. The shock of brine hits you first, then the cucumber and spring greens, a mouth-filling freshness you won't even try to translate into words. You'll just have another, lingering over the wet scent of the shell. Whoever said "You can't eat the view" clearly hadn't been here.

The sleet has turned to snow now, piling up against the foot of the A-frames, and you shiver a little as a draft finds its way into your refuge, but you are not at all unhappy. You are the opposite, whatever that is. A raft of scoter ducks floats by, diving for clams.

ROWAN JACOBSEN is the author of *A Geography of Oysters*, *The Essential Oyster*, *American Terroir* and other books. He has received awards from the James Beard Foundation, the Society of American Travel Writers and the Overseas Press Club. His podcast *Wild Chocolate* tells of searching the Amazon for lost varieties of wild cacao.

THREE POEMS

Written by **DUANE NIATUM**

S'KLALLAM SPIRIT CANOE

My paddle keeps to the sun's path,
pulls back home to sea,
my blood on its travels to the whirling depths.
From bow to stern our canoe drops and rises,
embraces each trough cleansed
by family singing from coastal cliffs.
We join our brothers' and sisters'
canoes from other villages
in the circle of kelp and spray,
seal and whale; ride the moving hills,
slide sideways and down, then straight up,
each paddle touching sky.

The drumbeat slips beneath the current,
rattles from genes to prow,
returns to ancestral fire and form
emerging from the trail of cutwater.

From dawn to night we are the ribs
of great grandparents, soar like cormorants
on the green crest; offer our children
a dream stronger and bolder than rage or war.

Salt drying on our face and hands braids
our bodies into spirals of dusk,
Evening Star and Milky Way, hones us
for the split hurdle as we speak
with night weavers like the old growth voice
of red cedar dipping into light
the mirror of our coming-home story.

JOURNEY TO HURRICANE RIDGE

The climb up the trail to the ridge
will be slow and steady,
the view acute and the passion outspread wings.
The sky point, setting the direction,
off the memory for breaking ground,
crosses our path like the osprey,
far above the cloud banks
floating within blue currents.
The dance hangs between day and night.
A black-capped chickadee in the red cedar eyes
Coyote drifting with the white-wave on the horizon.

The climb will be slow and steady,
strengthening us in a flow of sunlight
back down the mountain.
The nerves, elders of the blood,
trace their roots to the edge,
to rock, lichen and crow.
We have come to rest with the molecular,
the lava layers exposed to eternity.
when the veins pulsing in our toes
give themselves to the sky
we hear the earth's core shift.

With the sky pounding through our hearts,
the snow under our feet will shape
for our children the rivers
of these mountains and their songs
settled in our gene pools.
Guests of dead pines and spruce,
the wind breakers, the wind bleaches
us white as the sun.

Even the deer family we watched
near the forest and valley below
will leave footprints to chance
on the snow for others climbing beyond
themselves for the lost connection.
With bald eagle flying high in circles
and screeching wing notes in our blood
we touch earth to unknot the spine.

DIVING OFF THE KLALLAM COAST

Day

Near the rocks, the sea's legends break
in a choir of white caps beyond boats
and buoy, as the waves carve shells
down to green anemones.
I swim the reef and watch perch dive,
oyster move sand, sand move man.

Along the stone-age cliff, a diver's dream,
skeletons of seals reflect the layers of death.
I grow fonder of the sea as Thunderbird
peers from cave to soar in the sea wind,
like a dream riding the wind's back.
My arms now fins, I dive under a school
of moon jellyfish, flipping from their sting.
Blue bass slip away under sunlight.
A crab secure within the crevice of the reef
eyes me but is indifferent as the sun,
looking boldly with claws at attention.

A starfish crawls like the tide, always alert
to where a clam or oyster hides.
Leaving the jetty, the sea losing sun pours
time through the razor clam's shell
at orange-bending twilight.

Night

The sea's mosaic motion rolls into pine cliffs
And I step slowly over earth's cool edge.
Sounds lose themselves in madrona leaves.
Infinity's clandestine forest holds fast
To light and then to summer rains.
Luminous planets whirl over fish gardens
And seashells; sound stops; the moon passes
Over sea lilies, eelgrass, and mountains of hemlock.
Darkness shapeshifts, an eye of transparent stone.

Ferns fold themselves into waves of moonlight
As if children of the sky.
Ducks and gulls drift in a circle of calm,
Sleep like babies in a nest,
Rhyme with the changing of the evening,
winter's cave, no longer distant as the moon
at anchor, looms where mounds of shell and bones
sing of ancestors, the whalers' lost village
in the world. My soul burns a fire near the beach
for guardian spirits dancing and singing legends
of their forest, rising like eagle from the sea.

DUANE NIATUM [Jamestown S'Klallam Tribe] has been writing poems, stories and essays for over 60 years; published widely in the U.S. and abroad. His 10 books of poems include *Earth Vowels* and the latest, *Sea Changes*. The legends and traditions of his ancestors, who have long called this place home, help shape and animate his poetry.

THE TREE DETECTIVES

Written by **CIARA O'ROURKE**

THE SKY WAS CLEAR on the night of August 3, 2018, as three men donned headlamps and walked deeper into the woods on the Olympic Peninsula. Stepping between Douglas firs, ferns whispering at their feet, the trio finally skittered down a steep slope to a creek and stood before a hulking tree. A bigleaf maple loomed over them in the dark.

Shaggy with moss and soaring high into the forest canopy, bigleaf maples are the tallest maples in North America, growing upward of 100 feet. And for centuries they've drawn both man and beast to their trunks with sap that can be boiled down to a syrup and seeds that nourish the thrushes and sparrows that fly among their boughs. Indigenous peoples have long used the trees for medicinal purposes.

Bigleaf maples are also prized for their fine-grained wood. Some of the trees develop a coveted pattern that resembles rippling water. If you've ever watched guitarist Carlos Santana perform, you've likely seen a musical instrument crafted from this wood.

The grain and quality make bigleaf maples desirable in the world's markets for beautiful and singular woods. That value has spurred a criminal enterprise that's not unique to the Olympic Peninsula but is certainly well-suited to its moss-upholstered stands of massive trees. And crime in the woods, in turn, inspires a distinctive strand of research and detection.

* * *

The men approaching that bigleaf had been at work for months, felling trees on national forestland without a permit, cutting blocks of wood from their trunks and selling them to mill owners with a falsified permit that indicated the timber was legally harvested from private property. They planned to cut this maple too. Then they saw the bees.

A colony had found refuge among the huge tree's limbs, and one of the men—Shawn Williams, who went by "Thor"—was allergic. Williams had been hired by a fellow named Justin Wilke to help haul the wood out of the forest.Authorities would later say that Wilke tried blasting the nest with wasp killer. When that didn't work, prosecutors believe he doused it with gasoline and clicked open a lighter. A small fire snapped in the cold air, torching the hive until the men extinguished the flames with creek water and returned to their campsite. The tree would have to wait.

Fog settled on the forest early that morning, but that wasn't what drew the men's attention when they woke up. As they emerged from their tents, they saw smoke. The smoldering pile of ash they left behind had ignited, licking at the forest's understory, charring hemlock and burning through acre after acre until, eventually, 3,300 acres of forestland would succumb to flames. It would be more than two months before firefighters could contain the blaze and not until November that rainfall would snuff it for good.

The bigleaf maple tree somehow survived. But as investigators sifted through the wreckage, they discovered three other maples felled nearby, all chopped down with chunks carved out along the trunk, the most valuable wood poached from the tree with the remains left to rot, like a rhino killed and robbed of its horn.

The theft would have likely gone unnoticed were it not for the fire. Amid the vast wilderness on the Olympic Peninsula, someone would have had to both come upon these trees, off trail and realize they were looking at a crime scene. The woods are so dense you could stand within yards of a fallen tree and not realize it. Plus, the Olympic National Forest, which essentially surrounds the national park, sprawls to more than 633,600 acres. The Forest Service unit that manages it employs only one criminal investigator.

As the losses from the fire stacked up—$4 million in fire suppression, park trails closed, ecosystems singed, and Washingtonians choking on drifting smoke—authorities started looking for culprits. Eventually, they arrested Wilke and Williams.

Wilke denied that he started the fire, and a jury acquitted him of that particular accusation. But he admitted to cutting bigleaf maple trees in the forest. He was struggling to "get by," he says in —, a documentary about Wilke by University of Washington professors Lynn Thomas, Daniel Hoffman and Michael Sanderson. In the

film, Wilke, who lives in Shelton, a small town northwest of Oregon's capital, Olympia, describes a deep affinity for the forest and objects to the idea that he's not entitled to his share of it.

"Who is anybody to tell me I can't cut a tree down out in our woods?" he says. "That's our land. That's not the government's land—is it? Do you think George Washington would've said, 'Oh, prosecute him?' I don't think so. Our founding founders gave that land to us. The national forest is public land."

* * *

Alongside the wet, mythical wilderness of the Olympic Peninsula live people who don't necessarily have enough money to spend a week vacationing in the park—or to buy groceries, for that matter. In this landscape of natural riches and tight economies, tree poaching isn't a new phenomenon. In the early days of colonial settlement, rogue ships would station themselves off the peninsula to spirit away trees; in 2013, another Washington man was convicted for a tree-poaching spree that included the felling of a 300-year-old Douglas fir. In today's Olympic Peninsula, human and societal woes tend to fuel the practice.

"In my experience, the vast majority have serious drug addictions and are trying to fund that," says Seth Wilkinson, one of the federal attorneys who prosecuted Wilke and Williams. Stealing wood from the forest is thus perhaps a rural equivalent of some more urban styles of crime: Poachers wrest hunks of wood from maple trees the same way catalytic converters are sawed from Priuses parked on Seattle streets by those seeking their palladium and platinum. It's hard to haul wood out of the forest, and thieves will take only the highest value pieces and leave most of the tree behind.

The federal government began prosecuting accused tree poachers in the 1990s but, Wilkinson says, the cases are often stymied by suspects' contentions that the wood was harvested on private land—claims historically hard to disprove, especially if you don't have a stump. While in this case Williams pleaded guilty, Wilke stuck with this defense tactic. However, even before the fire that would lead to the charges against him, a project that would help convict him was underway.

* * *

Richard Cronn, a research geneticist with the U.S. Forest Service, studies tree DNA. In the late 2010s, Cronn was at work on a database of tree genetics that would enable investigators to match blocks of wood brought into mills with trees in specific regions of the forest. Using bigleaf maple stumps investigators found in the woods as they investigated the Maple Fire, Cronn could get even more specific: Some of the wood Wilke sold to a mill in Tumwater was a genetic match to the remains of those three felled trees discovered in the forest. The probability the match could have been a coincidence was infinitesimal—one in an undecillion. Put another way, that's a one in 1,000,000,000,000,000,000,000,000,000,000,000,000 chance.

It was the first time tree DNA evidence had been used in a federal criminal trial. Wilke was sentenced to 20 months in prison for crimes including conspiracy and trafficking unlawfully harvested timber, and Wilkinson believes this conviction will dissuade other would-be poachers from even trying. Anne Minden, who was an expert witness in Wilke's case, is also hopeful.

A special agent for the Forest Service from 1987 to 2014, Minden started investigating timber theft cases on the peninsula in the mid-1990s. She recalls a case in the aughts, in which a man from Hood Canal was out hunting and discovered multiple maple trees cut down in Olympic National Forest. The man who made this find was angry—he was a logger, and he wanted to know why the Forest Service hadn't solicited bids on the work, which he himself would have liked to have. He was complaining about it at a bar that night when a Forest Service employee overheard him and looked into the matter.

"Everything in the woods is worth something to someone," Minden says.

* * *

John Soltys and his daughter, Clara, drove from their home in North Bend one summer morning in 2018 bound for Toleak Point, a popular beach campsite in Olympic National Park, where waves crash against sea stacks and bald eagles circle overhead. Soltys and Clara, then 15, were planning to backpack along the Olympic Coast, but they had mapped out more than where they would sleep each night. Pulling over his old, and beat-up Subaru near a bigleaf maple grove, Soltys got out of the car and lifted the trunk to reveal what they had started to consider a miniature science lab.

Father and daughter were among more than 100 people participating in a project to pick bigleaf maple leaves for Adventure Scientists, a Bozeman, Montana-based group that gathers outdoors data to help address environmental problems. This particular initiative required volunteers to collect maple samples and measurements from Southern California to British Columbia so that scientists could build a database of tree DNA across the region with the aim of thwarting the illegal timber trade.

Capturing the circumference of the maples was often a two-person job. Soltys would grab one end of the tape measure, and Clara, the other, and they'd meet on the other side to gauge just how gigantic these trees were. Soltys and Clara, and often his other two children, regularly spent time exploring outside, and he thought these kinds of projects were a cool way to engage them with the natural world. But what started as an academic exercise began to feel even more meaningful when some of the data Adventure Scientists collected was used in the Maple Fire case.

Kaleb Madsen, a 36-year-old hydrologic engineer, wasn't aware of tree poaching before he volunteered to collect bigleaf maple samplesfor Adventure Scientists, driving along the peninsula's Hamma Hamma drainage in search of healthy trees.

"What was and is a passion for me is understanding and protecting our wild places," he says. "The forest and the mountains have always been my happy place."

Another volunteer dispatched to the peninsula, Jesse Brighten, has a personal history of trees. Brighten's father logged forests in the Pacific Northwest in the 1960s and '70s, while Brighten, 36, is an arborist living on Whidbey Island. His feelings about tree poachers like Wilke are complicated. He's empathetic to people struggling with addictions, and conscious of the economic disparities on the peninsula. And he has a hard time getting wound up about someone illegally harvesting trees while the government allows timber companies to clearcut swaths of forestland. But he hopes the DNA database will help target bigger poaching fish.

He and a colleague were driving to one bigleaf maple tree they had previously identified as a potential source for a sample when they

were stopped short. The road was closed and the air was smoky. The maple, as it turned out, was the tree Wilke and Williams had tried to cut down a few nights earlier. And it was on fire.

CIARA O'ROURKE has reported for *Seattle Metropolitan* as well as the *Austin American-Statesman, The Atlantic* and *The New York Times.* She was a 2015-2016 Ted Scripps Fellow in Environmental Journalism.

IRON MAN

From the *Tacoma News-Tribune*
May 1929

JOHN HUELSDONK, PIONEER HERCULES, WILL COME "OUTSIDE" HIS PENINSULA TO JOIN IN RAILROAD CELEBRATION

ABERDEEN. —John Huelsdonk, "the Iron Man of the Olympics," whose feats as a packer, hunter and all-around woodsman and pioneer have thrilled many a campfire group in the peninsula wilderness, will be a guest of honor at the railroad jubilee banquet here. Amid the glare of lights and happy ramblings of celebration speakers, Huelsdonk, the giant of a man whose trail strength knew no bounds, will commemorate in his own quiet way the realization of a lifetime dream—a railroad. For the proposed Olympic line, Grays Harbor to the Hoh River, is just what Huelsdonk has waited for.

Grown gray in his long vigil in the wilderness, the barrel-checked Hoh River pioneer will be able to reflect on 38 years of toil in the wildest and most remote valley in the state.

Huelsdonk thinks nothing of the feats that are a constant source of wonder even to other hardened pioneers. He does not see anything remarkable in his ability, in younger days, to pack two men's burden on his broad back. He does not realize that to others he is a man of reverence for his feat of carrying a kitchen range on his back from Forks to his homestead, 22 miles.

These facts are vouched for and certified. Fifteen years ago, when the trails into the upper Hoh were being built, Huelsdonk would strap 175 pounds on his back and pack it up to the trail crews. He did this not for bravado, but for two men's pay. And two men's pay through the short working season helped send his four daughters through the university.

PACKED COOK STOVE

And there is the time that a forest ranger met him on the trail near T. R. H. Schmidt's place, on the way from Forks to the Huelsdonk ranch. The big settler had a cook stove on his back, and was trudging unconcernedly down

the forest aisle. The ranger made the remark that "that must be quite a load, eh, John?"

"Well," Huelsdonk replied in all sincerity, "it isn't so bad, only there is a sack of flour in the oven that keeps shifting around and unsettling this load."

This sort of pioneer Hercules or Jean Val Jean settled in the Hoh in 1891 at the age of 22. A year later he made a visit to Iowa, got married and brought his bride out to the forest home. She loved the place from the first, has been "outside" only once since. They came out for the Seattle fair, but Mrs. Huelsdonk was so bored by civilization that she vowed that "they would never get her out there again." She is known far and wide as the best cook on the peninsula.

DAUGHTERS TEACH

Their four daughters are often at home with the old folk. Two of them, Mrs. Fred Fletcher and Mrs. John Fletcher, live near the mouth of the Hoh, a day's hike from the homestead. Dora and Marie teach school. For several years they have spent the early summer months catching elk calves for shipment to other ranges and for exhibition at sportsmen's shows. They say that the elk are now too numerous for the limited winter range and that the depopulation in this manner is the most humane method of solving the problem.

At 61, John Huelsdonk, despite his gray beard, retains the magnificent physique which made his prowess a legend along the Olympic trails. His great torso tells of wilderness toil, not yet over with, but to be eased by a railroad in his declining years. The big rancher has been in Aberdeen once in his 38 years on the Olympic Peninsula. He makes regular trips out to Forks, but seldom goes farther.

When the railroad reaches the Hoh, he will be able to ship his cattle and turkeys to market by train instead of driving them over an arduous trail.

When Huelsdonk "comes out" this time, he will see some startling things. He will see, for the first time, modern automobiles. He will see airplanes, while electric lights and street cars are no familiar sights to him.

JOHN HUELSDONK, [1866-1947] was born in the German principality of Lippe. He lived most of his life in the rain-drenched Hoh. His deeds as "the Iron Man of the Hoh" made him a backcountry legend. Seven years after the publication of this article, he killed the largest cougar ever seen on the Peninsula.

DIRECTORY
& INDEX

DIRECTORY

LODGING

Arctic Club *Seattle*
Bishop Hotel *Port Townsend*
Captain Whidbey Inn *Whidbey Island*
Commodore *Astoria*
Hobuck Beach Resort *Neah Bay*
Hoh Valley Cabins *Forks*
Kalaloch Lodge *Forks*
KEX *Portland*
Lake Crescent Lodge *Lake Crescent*
Log Cabin Resort *Lake Crescent*
LOGE *Westport*
Long Beach Campfield *Long Beach*
Mike's Beach Resort *Hood Canal*
Mossquatch Resort *Forks*
Olympic Lodge *Port Angeles*
Quileute Oceanside Resort *La Push*
Quinault Lodge *Lake Quinault*
Sol Duc Hot Springs Resort *Sol Duc*
Sou'Wester *Seaview*
Starrett House *Port Townsend*
Sunrise Resort *Hoodsport*
Tokeland Hotel *Toke Point*

OUTFITTERS

Adventures Through Kayaking *Port Angeles*
Alpha Angler *La Push*
Broken Spoke *Port Townsend*
Center for Wooden Boats *Seattle*
Elevate Outdoors Port *Angeles*
Hurricane Ridge Winter Sports Association *Hurricane Ridge*
La Push Surf Adventures *La Push*
Métier Racing & Coffee *Seattle*
Mike Z's Guide Service *Forks*
Miyar Adventures *Seattle*
Mountain Shop *Portland*
Next Adventure *Portland*
Northwest Alpine Guides *Sedro-Wooley*
Northwest Maritime Center *Port Townsend*
Olympic Hiking Company *Port Angeles*
Olympic Kayak Tours *Port Townsend*
Olympic Mountain Guiding *Sequim*
Pacific Alpine Guides *Winthrop*
REI *Seattle, etc.*
Sail Port Townsend *Port Townsend*
Seattle Boat Works *Seattle*
Sound Bikes & Kayak *Port Angeles*
Steepwater *Westport*
Waters West *Port Angeles*
Windsong Charters *Neah Bay*
Windward Adventures *Seattle*
YSS Dive *Hoodsport*

ARTS & CULTURE

Browser's Bookstore *Olympia*
Burke Museum *Seattle*
Gray Coast Guildhall *Quilcene*
House of Myths Carving Shed *Sequim*
Imprint Bookstore *Port Townsend*
K Records *Olympia*
Killrockstars Records *Olympia*
Last Word Books *Olympia*
Makah Cultural and Resource Center *Neah Bay*
Northwest Native Expressions *Sequim*
Northwind Art *Port Townsend*
Olympic Driftwood Sculptors *Sequim*
Port Book and News *Port Angeles*
Port Townsend School of Woodworking *Port Townsend*
Suquamish Museum *Suquamish*
Westport Maritime Museum *Westport*
William James Bookseller *Port Townsend*

INDEX

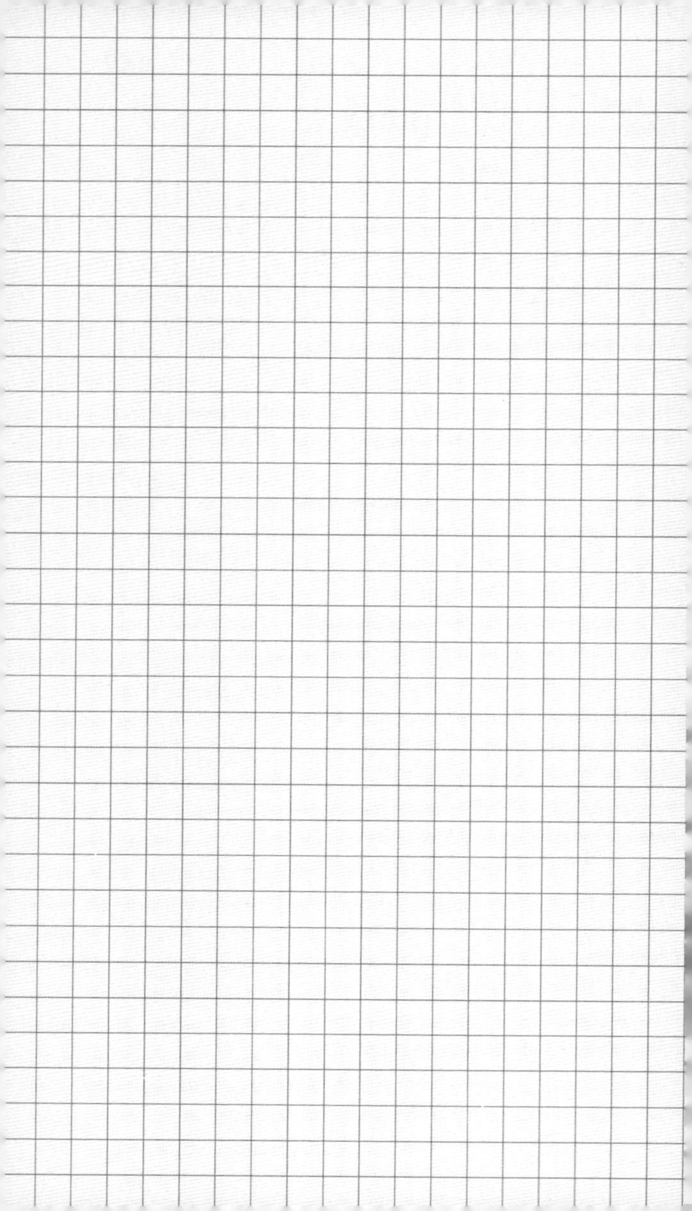